初中版

STEM创想家

孔云峰　主编

中英双语版

江苏凤凰科学技术出版社

图书在版编目（C I P）数据

STEM创想家：初中版. 4 / 孔云峰主编. -- 南京：
江苏凤凰科学技术出版社, 2019.7
ISBN 978-7-5713-0492-8

Ⅰ. ①S… Ⅱ. ①孔… Ⅲ. ①科学知识－初中－教学
参考资料 Ⅳ. ①G634.73

中国版本图书馆CIP数据核字(2019)第147982号

STEM 创想家　初中版 4

主　　编	孔云峰
责任编辑	卢海春
责任校对	郝慧华
责任监制	曹叶平　周雅婷
出版发行	江苏凤凰科学技术出版社
出版社地址	南京市湖南路1号A楼，邮编：210009
出版社网址	http：//www.pspress.cn
印　　刷	溧阳市金宇包装印刷有限公司
开　　本	889mm × 1194mm　1/16
印　　张	5.5
版　　次	2019年7月第1版
印　　次	2019年7月第1次印刷
标准书号	ISBN 978-7-5713-0492-8
定　　价	35.00元

编者寄语

少年儿童是可爱的，是活泼的。少儿时期，每一个人都有各种各样奇奇怪怪的念头。用这套书的标题来说就是：每一个人都是创想家！

学习 STEM 真好玩。STEM 听起来好像很难，但究其本意却十分平常，因为我们的生活、我们身边的事物，都蕴含着科学原理（S），都有技术设计（T），都体现了工程精华（E），也都有跟数学（M）相关的话题。

不言而喻，《STEM 创想家》是非常有价值的，对少年儿童的学习成长十分有帮助。为什么呢？因为有趣的知识为少年儿童打开了创想的窗户，因为有意思的活动将少年儿童带进了 STEM 的殿堂……引导少年儿童并不容易，这可是充满“专业”的工作啊！本书的作者们都有着丰富的教学经验，他们将最得意的作品奉献给少年儿童。

我们相信，孩子们一定会喜爱上《STEM 创想家》，也一定会赢得老师们和家长们的点赞。因为它凝聚了年轻教育工作者令人赞叹的激情和智慧，因为它能帮助少年儿童更加健康地成长！

作者简介

孔云峰

从事中小学科学教育工作，曾任小学科学教研员，现任中学科学教研员。于 2006 年公派赴法接受“做中学”培训，曾多次指导教师获得上海市中青年教师教学评比一、二等奖。

任海芸

任教于上海市华东模范中学，担任化学、科学教学任务。中学一级教师，上海市化工学会会员。擅长特色班、竞赛辅导教学和双语教学。教学中注重学科应用，引导学生通过探究获取知识，积累了实验教学经验。

胡　菁

初中科学学科教学经验丰富，能制定符合学生个性特点的授课方案。拥有5年物理、化学、科学实验员经验，熟知三门学科中演示、学生实验器材准备和实验过程，能够独立制作、研发、改进实验器材。

陈秀英

从事高中物理、初中物理和科学教学近 25 年。对 STEM 课程有浓厚的兴趣和研究热情，曾撰写校本拓展课《科学小实验》。曾多次指导学生荣获高中物理全国竞赛二等奖以及“白猫杯”化学竞赛一、二、三等奖。

葛　艳

从事初中化学、科学教学工作 17 年，中学高级教师，上海市教育学会中小学科学教学专业委员会成员，曾获上海市中小学中青年教师教学评选活动二等奖。多次带领指导学生参加各类科技制作评比活动，获一、二、三等奖。

一分钟了解璞远 STEM

STEM 是科学 (Science)、技术 (Technology)、工程 (Engineering) 和数学 (Mathematics) 四门学科的简称，强调多学科的交叉融合，将四门学科内容组合形成有机整体，以更好地培养学生的创新思维与实践能力。

以项目为抓手，将学科知识渗透到项目中去，注重孩子学科知识整合和解决实际问题的能力。注重兴趣学习，培养综合能力，让孩子保持好奇心。保有学习动机才是孩子未来的竞争力。

璞远 STEM 研发团队由幼儿园、小学、中学的中外名师汇集。

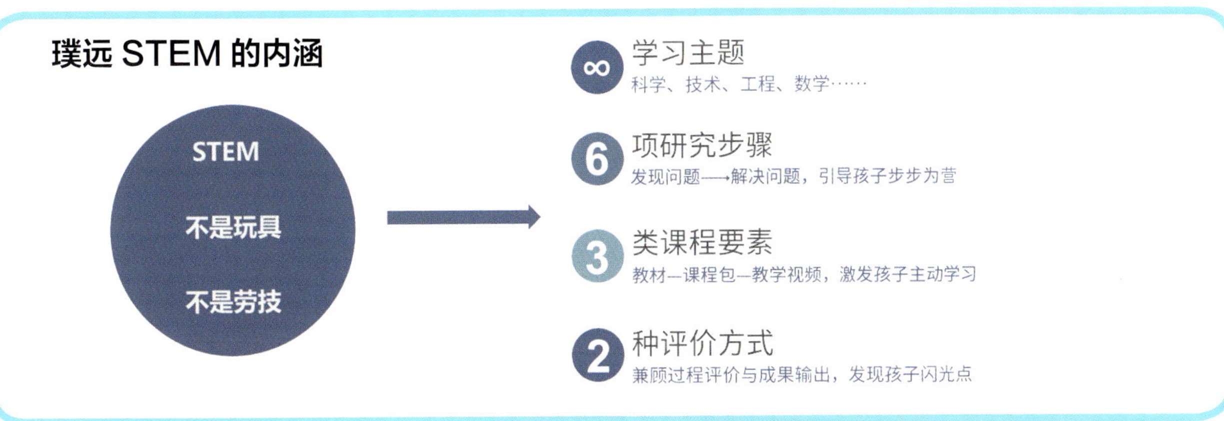

研发理念

融合美国、澳洲、欧洲STEM经典课程

依据《中小学国家课程标准》

围绕科学精神和创新能力展开

K—12（幼儿园—小学—中学）

全学段中英双语课程体系

激发孩子探究科学世界，学习数理知识的兴趣和热情

为孩子搭建系统而坚实的数学、物理、化学、生物与自然科学的知识结构

训练孩子手脑协调，学习与实践结合，发现问题、主动研究、解决问题的能力

不同梯度设置

II 探究拓展班

(8~11 岁) 小学3~5年级

IV 国际竞赛班

(15~20岁) 9年级至大学

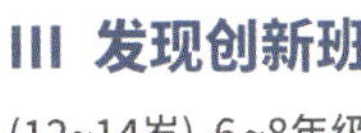

III 发现创新班

(12~14岁) 6~8年级

I 低幼启蒙班

(4~7岁) 幼儿园中班、大班、小学1~2年级

教研合作机构

华师大二附中浦东实验学校

上海金诚专修学院

观看教学视频，请扫二维码

CONTENT 目录

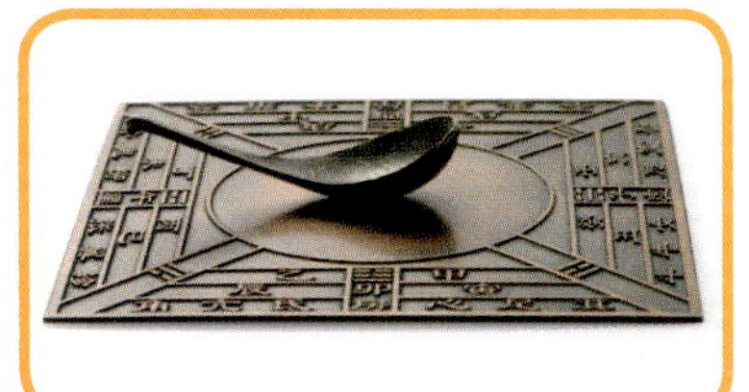

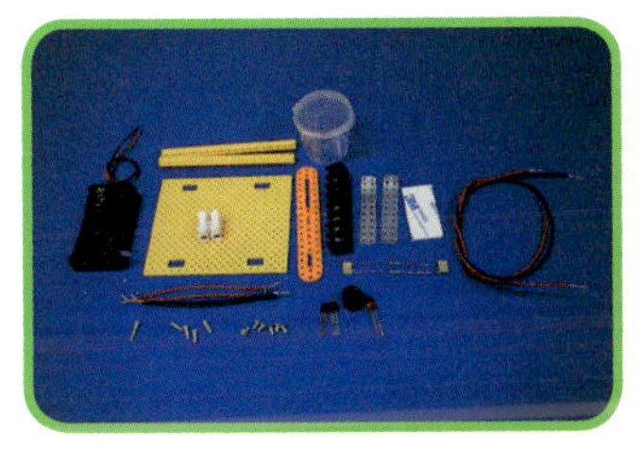

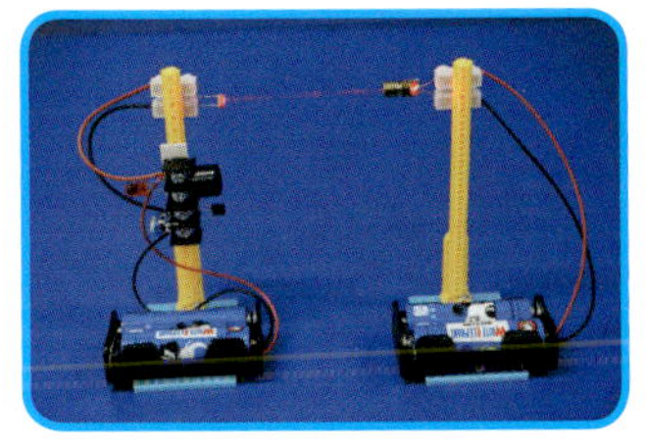

第一课 指南针

指南针是我国古代四大发明之一，也称司南。大家知道，指南针能指向南北方向，因此我们可以用它来辨别方向。

那么，你知道指南针为什么能指向南北方向吗？原来，指南针其实是一个小磁体，有南(S)、北(N)两极，而我们生活的地球是一个大磁体，也有南(S)、北（N）两极。地球产生的磁场类似于条形磁铁产生的磁场，如下图。

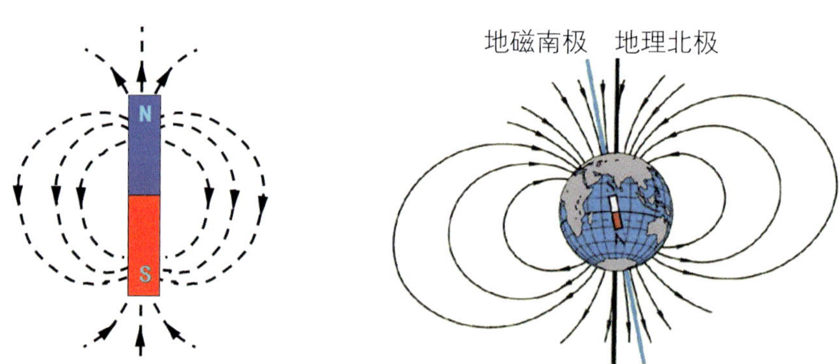

我们知道磁极（磁性最强处）之间的相互作用是同名磁极相斥、异名磁极相吸。指南针在地磁场的作用下，N 极会被地球磁场的 S 极吸引，S 极会被地球磁场的 N 极吸引。小磁针的 N 极指向地磁南极，恰是地球的地理北极的方向；S 极指向地磁北极，恰是地球的地理南极的方向。所以，指南针有了南北指向。可以说指南针是利用地球的磁场来辨别方向的。由图我们也可以知道，地球的地理南（北）极和地磁南（北）极是颠倒的。

实际上，地磁南（北）极和地理南（北）极还有一个夹角，我们称为磁偏角。不同地点的磁偏角是不一样的，在我国磁偏角一般情况下在2~6度。

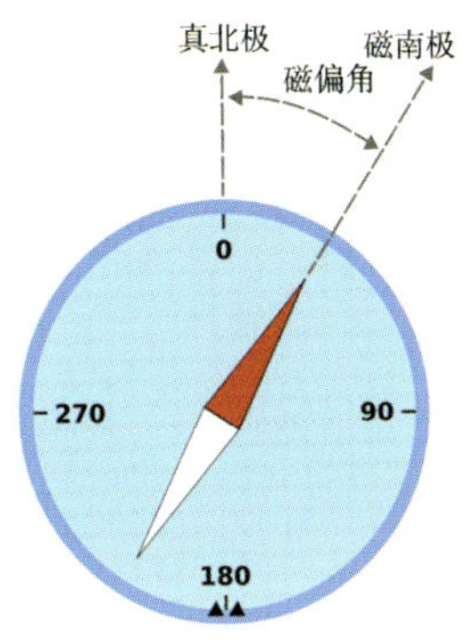

知道了指南针指向南北极的原理后，你能自己制作一枚指南针吗？

STEM实践：自制指南针

科学　知道磁铁的基本特性——有指向性；

技术　能够使用磁铁打磨其他物体，使其具有磁性；

工程　学会自制简单的指南针；

数学　了解指南针的作用，知道面和线的概念。

目标

1. 知道地球是一个大磁体。
2. 知道磁极间的相互作用，小磁针磁极的指向。
3. 知道磁化和退磁。
4. 能动手制作简易且可应用的指南针。

材料

大号缝衣针、条形磁铁、细线、培养皿、塑料薄膜、泡沫塑料等。

流程

1. 用条形磁铁的一极在缝衣针上从针尾到针尖沿同一方向移动 30~50 次，磁化缝衣针。

2. 可将针悬挂起来，待针静止时，针尖指向为南方。(注意条形磁铁要拿远一些)

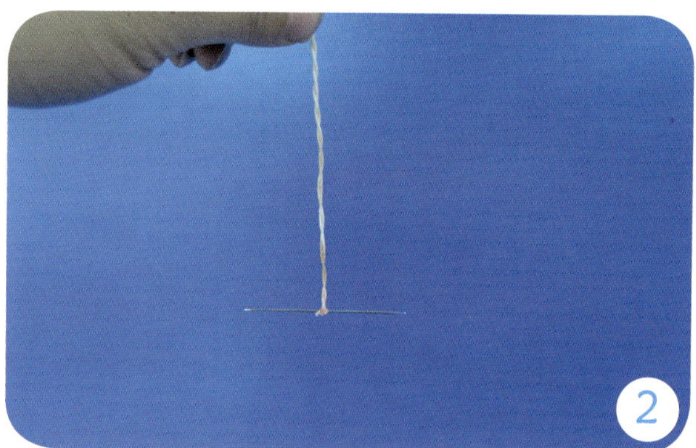

3. 也可将磁化的针放在泡沫塑料上，放在培养皿的水面上，无论你怎么放，最终静止时，针尖依然指向南方。

4. 或将磁化的针放在塑料薄膜上，一起放在培养皿里的水面上，针尖指向南方。用手旋转培养皿，缝衣针针尖依然指向南方。

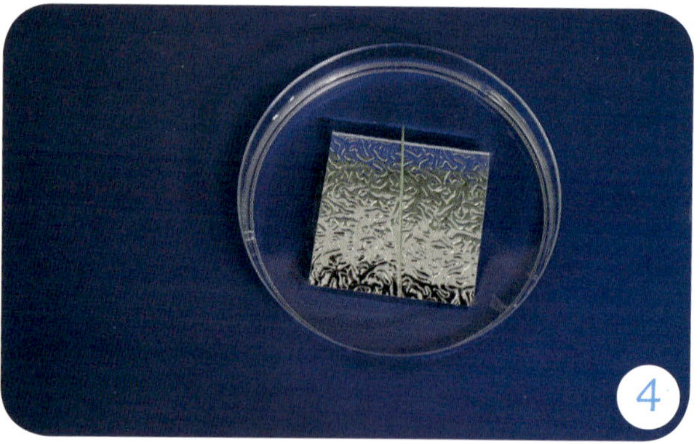

拓展

将一定量铁粉放入自封袋中，在自封袋的表面放上磁铁，观察现象，用铁粉分布的规律解释其中的科学原理。

第二课　土木工程

基础设施是为一个国家服务的所有基本系统，它使所有的运输和经济活动正常运行。它包括道路、桥梁、隧道、下水道、电网、供水和通信（包括互联网）等。

桥梁是基础设施的重要组成部分。是由工程师和工人们根据项目计划共同建造的。建造桥梁不是一件简单的工作。桥的外观很重要，但安全才是最重要的，所以，桥梁工程必须要进行设计和测试，在几个月的时间里，工程人员进行设计、测试、模拟、再设计，直到确定项目会成功。

桥梁是庞大的建筑，有的桥梁有几千米长、几百米高。成千上万的零件是由钢铁和混凝土等材料制成的。在桥上，可能共有几万吨重的小汽车、卡车、公共汽车和火车压在上面，有各种各样的力作用在桥梁上，比如重力、压力、张力……这就是为什么工程师在设计过程中必须使用物理知识来计算和处理桥梁的受力问题。

各种力示意图

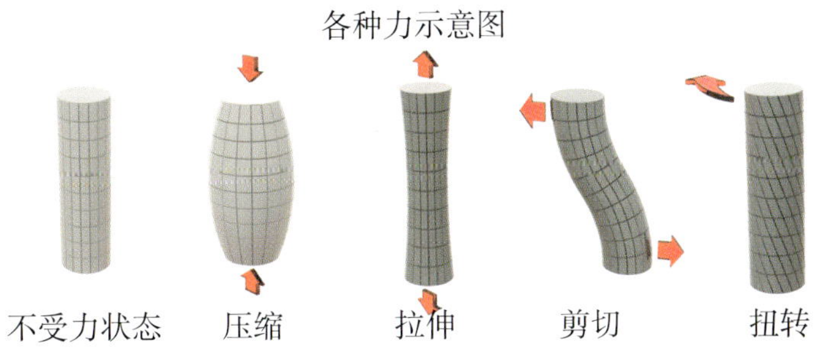

桥梁首先会受到重力，重力会影响所有的零件，产生相应的压力和张力。

压力是一种材料内部挤压的力。一些物体受到压力时会收缩，比如面包。较硬的物体能接受适度的压力，但如果压力强度太大，它就会断裂。像这样的事情发生时，会以不可预知的方式发生，因为很难确切知道薄弱的环节在哪里。

张力是一种反向的力——它向外伸展。例如，有些物体在被压缩时就会膨胀，就像气球一样。许多材料可以抵抗一些拉伸，事实上，适度的张力可以使材料更坚固。你见过杂技演员走钢丝吗？如果钢丝没有张力，钢丝和那个可怜的杂技演员都会掉下来！但是，太多的张力也会导致材料自身撕裂。考虑到桥梁所有部分发生的压力和张力，我们需要平衡这些力，并以一种安全的方式控制它们，如何做到这一点呢？

多年来，工程师们一直使用桁架结构，这是非常有效和安全的解决方案。如果你仔细观察一座桥——以旧金山金门大桥为例，你会发现许多形状，尤其是三角形。三角形被称为“最稳固的形状”，因为它的特性使得它在平衡压力、张力方面非常出色。

桁架就是一种结合了 5 个或 5 个以上三角形单元的结构，以某种方式使结构（例如桥梁或屋顶）组合表现为单个对象。这是一种有效的方法，用来平衡作用于物体上的力，比如重力、作用于物体组件上的压力和张力。

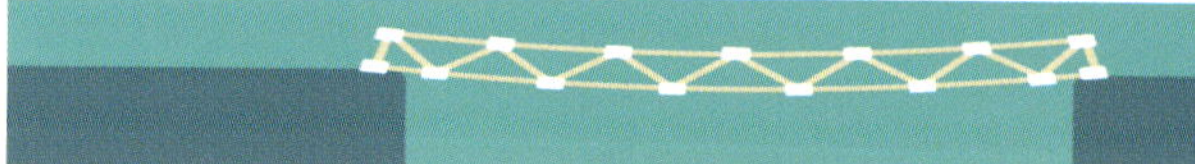

建筑师和工程师还必须考虑很多其他问题，比如暴风雪、风、地震，甚至交通。许多力都需要控制。任何一个力在一个点上变得太强，整个桥都可能会倒塌。这就是为什么要花很长的时间进行测试和修复预测到的问题。当你试着建造自己的桥梁时，你会亲身体验到这一点。注意故障点在哪里，然后进行更改以修复问题。一步一步，你将制作出一个伟大的成品！

STEM 实践：制作桁架桥

科学 建造东西时，必须要处理它所要承受的力；

技术 基础设施属于技术，建筑要依靠机器和材料来建造；

工程 工程不仅是建筑，还是整个设计和决策的过程；

数学 为了保证这座桥的安全性，需要了解它的几何形状并计算其受力。

目标

1. 了解力的概念以及力在工程和设计上的重要作用。
2. 知道张力、压缩、剪切、扭转之间的不同。
3. 了解一个工程的形状和设计与安全性、稳定性和耐久性有很大的关联。

材料

数根大小不一的木棒（10 cm、15 cm、20 cm）、泡沫塑料球、木条、用来测试的重物等。

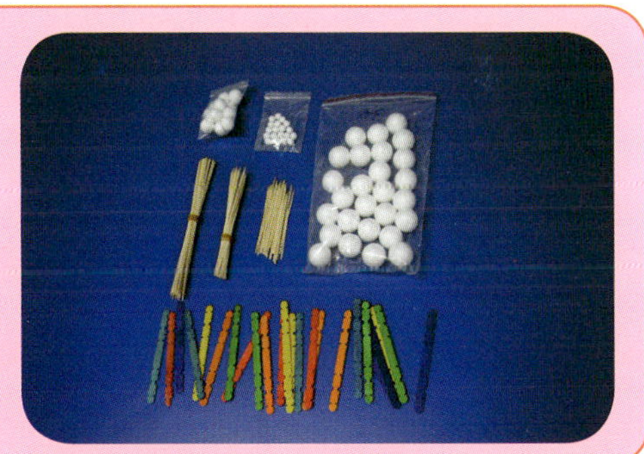

流程

1. 将木棒连接到泡沫塑料球上，构建一个基本的三角形框架结构。不要太用力地刺穿，避免损坏泡沫球。

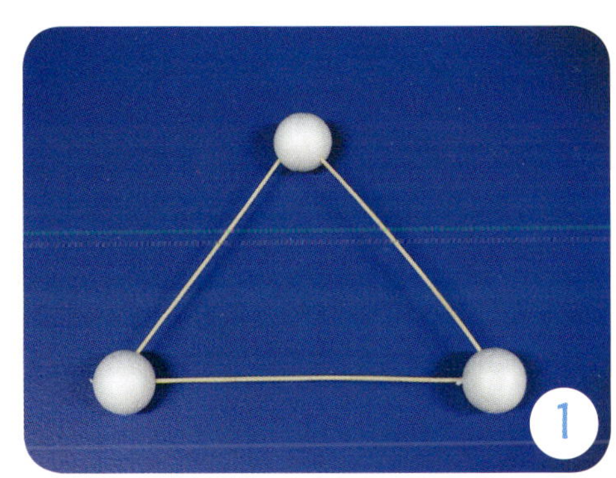

2. 复制你所构建的结构，使你的框架立体起来。注意角度。

3. 继续建造，用木棒将越来越多的结构连接整合在一起。

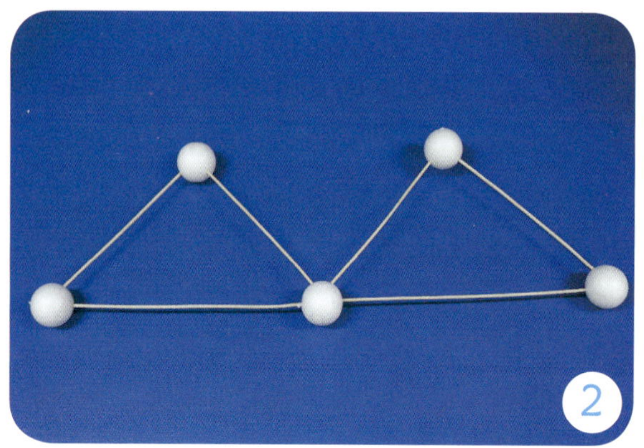

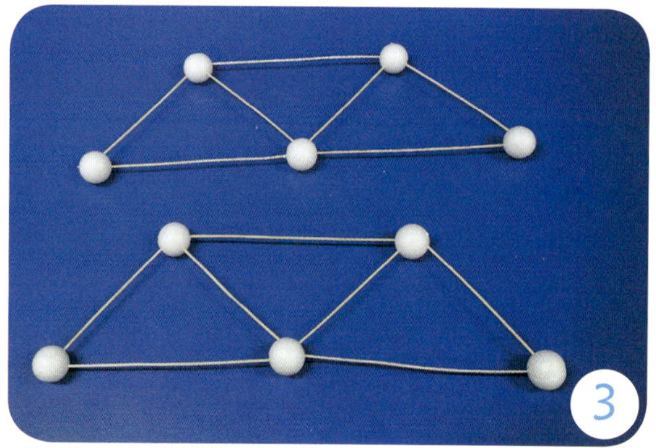

4. 在其中一个侧面结构上垂直插入短木棒，注意角度。

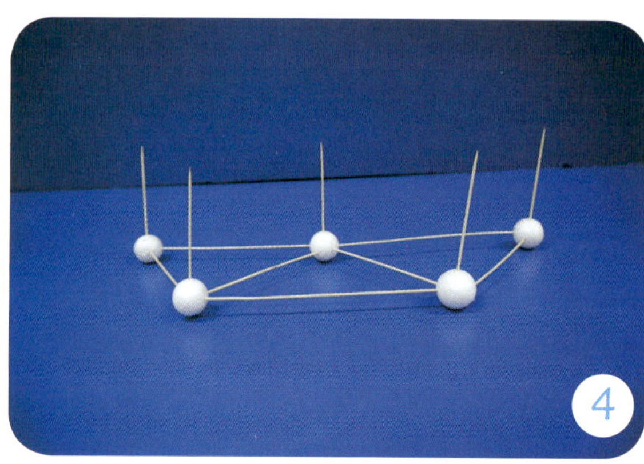

5. 相互组合，完成桥梁框架结构的搭建。仔细观察桥有可能倒塌的地方，你能看到压力和张力导致的一些问题吗？找出你需要纠正的地方。

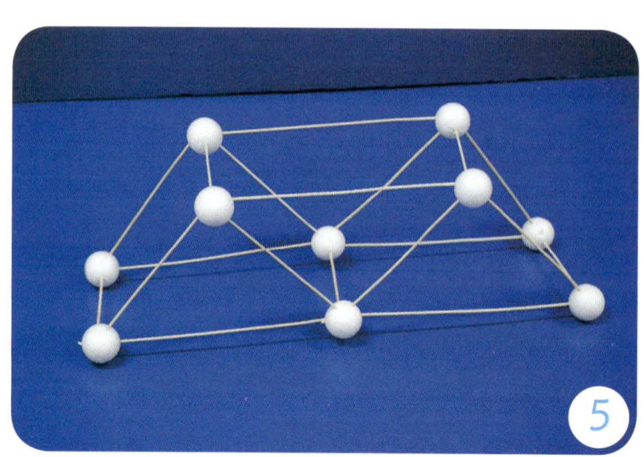

6. 在桥梁底部铺上木条，完成桥梁工程的搭建。构建好你的桥之后，通过在主平面上放置一些重物来进行测试。想象有一列很重的火车经过，这座桥会不会在一个点上坏了？看看你能做些什么来避免这种情况。

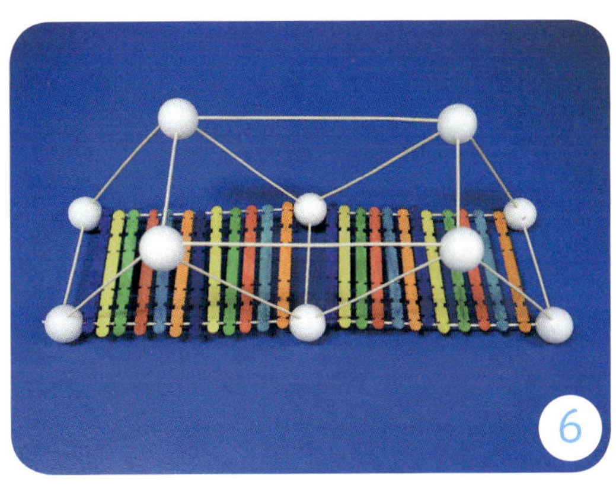

6

7. 用更多的材料来搭建更宏伟的桥梁。你要怎样支撑这座桥？只在两端支撑吗？下面需要有其他支柱来支撑吗？能把它建在两张桌子之间的空隙上吗？

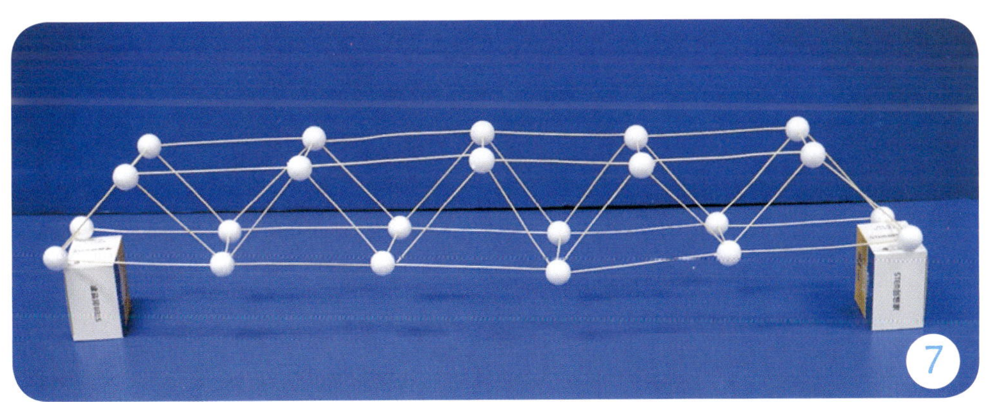

7

拓展

你可以把连接泡沫球的木棒剪短，这样可以解决一些棘手的问题。如搭建等边三角形、等腰三角形或斜角三角形，来帮助构造所需的形状。如果泡沫球因使用次数过多而损坏，最好将其更换掉。

第三课　湿度感应器

在人潮拥挤的公共场所，为实现温度和湿度的动态平衡，使设备、公众空间始终处于舒适、合理的环境中，工程师通常会在新风系统中加装湿度感应器，以帮助工作人员获取实时环境参数。生活中，在气象观测、植物栽培、文物管理、纸张制造等过程中都能发现湿度感应器的身影。

什么是湿度感应器

那么，科学家是如何通过一个简单的设备将湿度指标转换为电信号，实现感应报警功能的呢？简单地说，湿度感应器主要是利用三极管把通过人体、水等有湿度物体的电信号进行放大，经过放大后变成控制信号来控制 LED 灯的发光与蜂鸣器的声响。

实验电路的原理

科学家在一块半导体基片上制作两个相距很近的 PN 结，两个 PN 结把整块半导体分成三部分，中间部分是基区，两侧部分是发射区和集电区，排列方式有 PNP 和 NPN 两种。

图 1 为我们展示了 PNP 和 NPN 三极管电流方向的区别。三极管的三极分别是：E（或 e）发射极、B（或 b）基极和 C（或 c）集电极。如果将三极管作为开关使用，以 PNP 三极管为例，只有 b 极接上“电源 -”，e 极到 c 极才能够导通；相反，b 极不接线或接“电源 +”时，e 极到 c 极为关闭状态，此时 b 极需要接电阻以限制通过 b 极的电流。b 极与 e 极的电流若超出额定电流会导致三极管迅速升温，造成三极管输出不稳定，从而损坏三极管。

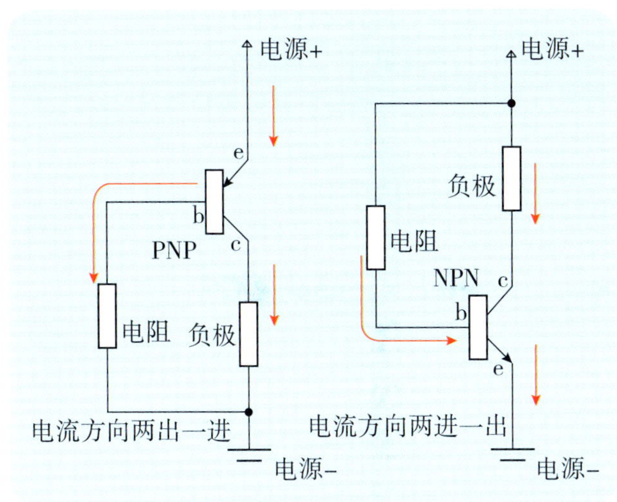

图 1

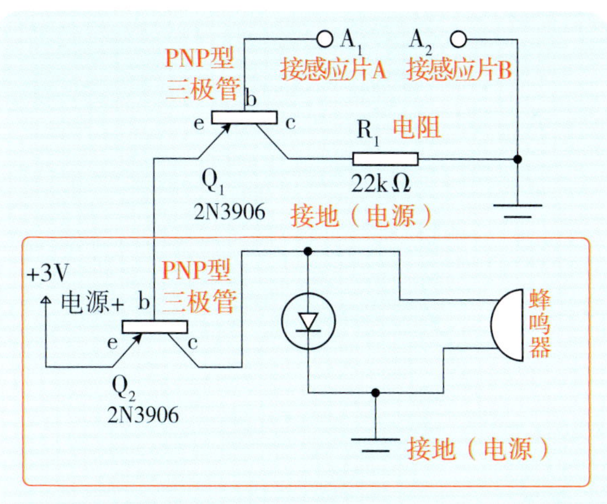

图 2

图2是本实验的电路图，主要采用两个PNP三极管对感应片的信号进行放大。实线框内是信号放大的执行电路，只要Q2三极管的b极导通到Q1的c极，Q2的e极到c极就会导通，点亮发光二极管，同时触发蜂鸣器。

实线框外为感应信号放大电路，Q1三极管把A1的信号放大使得Q1的e极到c极导通接地，并同时使Q2的b极到Q1的c极导通。反之，如果A1没有信号，那么Q1三极管的e极到c极则处于关闭状态，Q2也不会导通。

实验还隐藏了一个检测通路。电路中Q1的b极接通A1端口，A2端口接地，那么只要将A1与A2相连，整个电路即为闭合状态。因此，在使用湿度感应器时，需要用一个待检测的电阻导体将A1与A2隔开，如人体、一张干燥或湿润的纸、一块土等。这些物体的电阻通常很大。

湿度感应器是如何工作的

同时捏住A1与A2的感应片将A1、A2导通。电流通过Q1三极管，对A1的信号进行放大，进而使Q1的e极到c极导通。同理，Q2对Q1的信号又进行了一次放大，导通Q2的e极到c极。经过两次放大的电信号足以触发发光二极管和蜂鸣器。

STEM 实践：制作湿度感应器

科学 了解一些基本的电子元器件；

技术 学会按电路图组装电子元器件；

工程 能够组装湿度感应器；

数学 理清各元器件之间组装的顺序。

目标

1. 认识半导体元件——晶体三极管。
2. 了解晶体三极管在电路中的作用。
3. 了解此电路的工作原理。
4. 了解此电路可应用在哪些电路工程中。

材料

多孔底座、螺丝、螺丝帽、接线器、电池盒（含电池）、栅栏式接线端子、金属片、塑料片、蜂鸣器、LED 灯、三极管、电阻、导线、塑料杯、双面胶等。

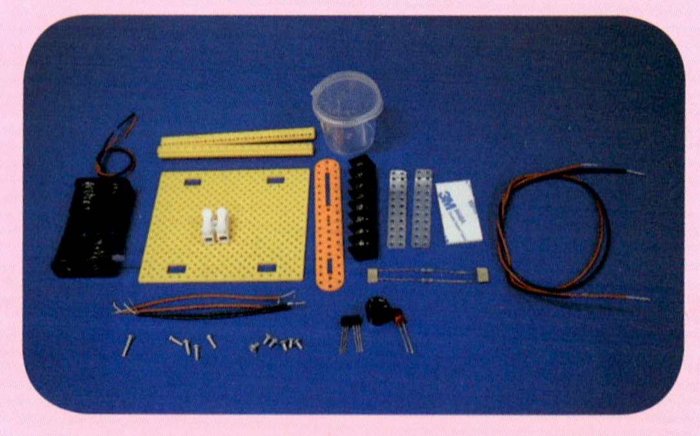

流程

1. 参照图 1 孔位，用 7 mm 螺丝把底座装好。

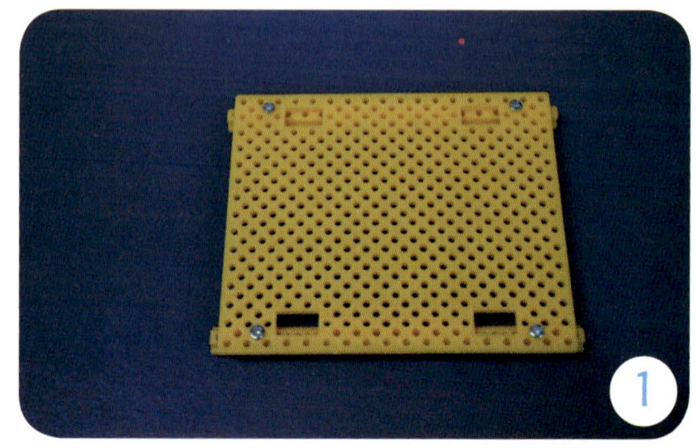

2. 参照图 2，把电池盒用 4 mm 螺丝固定在底座上，把一个白色的接线器用 10 mm 螺丝固定在底座左边，并剪取大小合适的双面胶把栅栏式接线端子粘到底座上端。

2

3. 仔细观察电路连接示意图，注意区分电子元器件的正极、负极和电路连接。

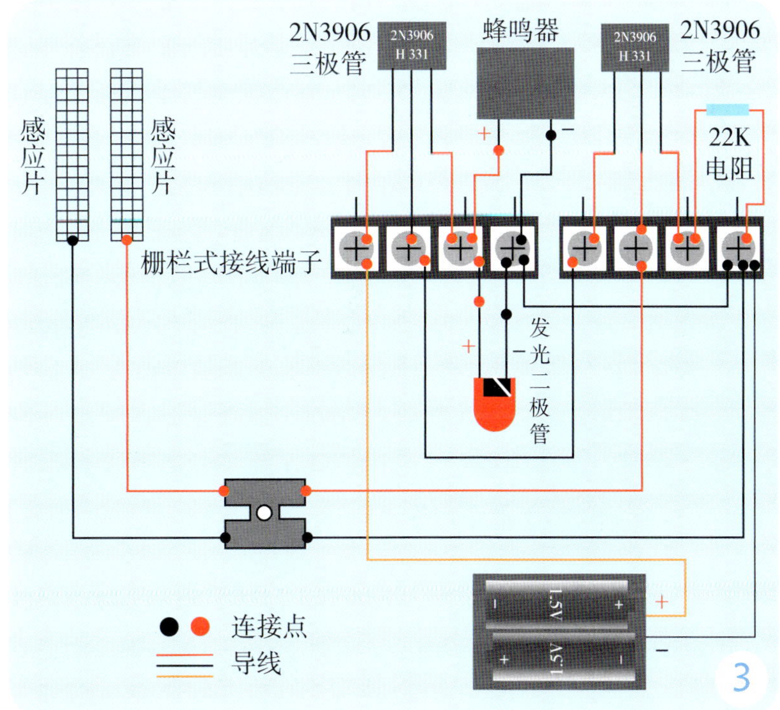

3

4. 按照电路示意图所示，首先将三极管字母朝上安装于栅栏式接线端子，然后将蜂鸣器和 LED 灯安装于栅栏式接线端子，再安装电阻，电阻不分正、负极，最后完成电路的接线。

5. 参照图 5，把金属片用 4 mm 螺丝安装在塑料片上，同时把长 40 cm 的红色导线的线芯卡在螺丝帽下方并固定好。

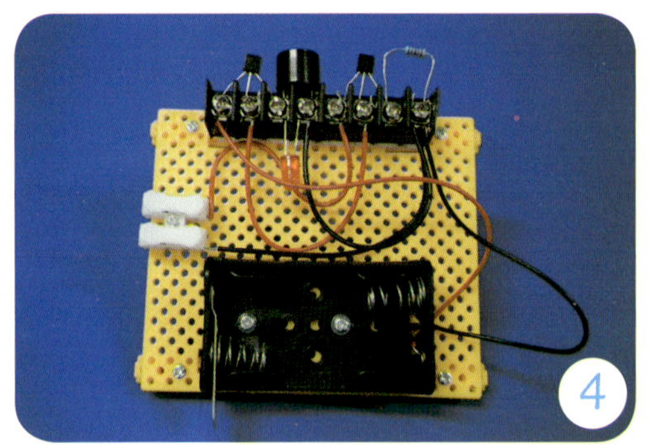
4

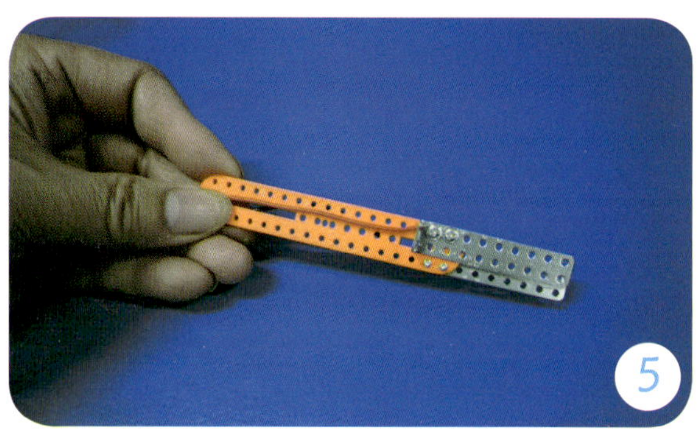
5

6. 参照图 6，把金属片用 4 mm 螺丝安装在塑料片的另一面上，同时把长 40 cm 的黑色导线的线芯卡在螺丝帽下方并固定好。

7. 把感应片的红、黑导线卡入白色的接线端子，湿度感应装置组装完成。在塑料杯中准备一杯水，然后把感应片装置放入水中，此时 LED 灯会亮起，蜂鸣器会响，证明湿度感应器能够正常工作。

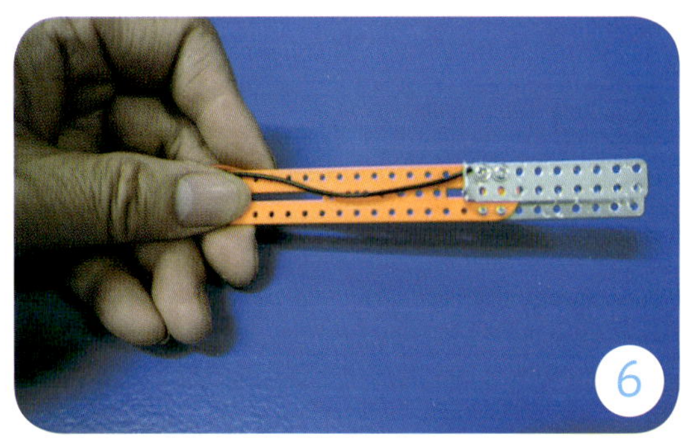
6

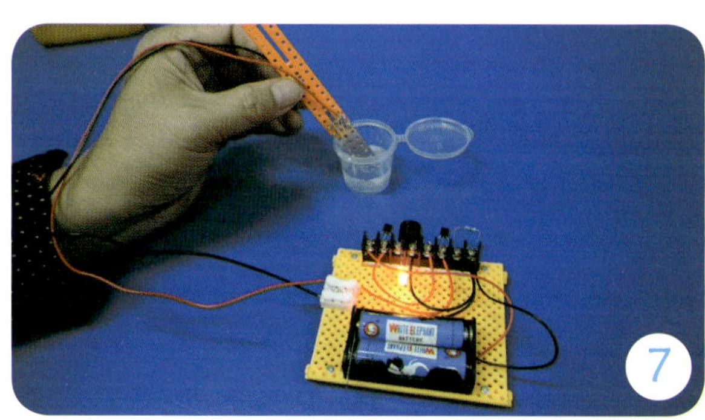
7

拓展

如果你能加上湿度传感器，那么你就能够控制 LED 灯在什么湿度条件下才会亮起来，湿度感应器的作用就更大了。

第四课　自制酸碱指示剂

生活中的溶液

在我们的日常生活中，会用到许多种溶液。有的是喝的，如天然矿泉水、汽水、橙汁、各类茶饮料等；有的是用来调味的，如酱油、醋等；有的是用来洗涤的，如各类洗衣液、洗手液、漱口水等；有的是家庭药用品，如碘酒、眼药水等。

这些日常生活中接触到的溶液哪些是酸性的？哪些是碱性？哪些又是中性的呢？我们应如何鉴别呢？

酸碱指示剂

酸碱指示剂有三种：紫色石蕊试液、无色酚酞试液和pH试纸。我们可以利用它们来测定溶液的酸碱性。紫色石蕊试液遇酸性溶液变红色，遇碱性溶液变蓝色，遇中性溶液不变色，所以紫色石蕊试液可以区分出酸、碱性溶液；无色酚酞试液只有遇碱性溶液变红色，所以它只能区分出碱性溶液；pH试纸是我们经常用到的酸碱指示剂，因为它既能知道溶液的酸碱性，还能知道溶液酸碱性的强弱。

那么在日常生活中，我们是否可以自己制作酸碱指示剂呢？

STEM 实践：自制酸碱指示剂

科学 知道用酸碱指示剂来测定溶液的酸碱性；

技术 能用常见的材料制作酸碱指示剂，并应用于检验日常用的溶液的酸碱性；

工程 完成酸碱指示剂制作；

数学 学会浓度配比和时间控制。

目标

1. 了解不同类型的酸碱指示剂。
2. 知道酸碱指示剂与溶液起化学反应，由颜色变化来判定溶液的酸碱性。
3. 能动手制作酸碱指示剂。
4. 能用制作好的酸碱指示剂来测定未知溶液的酸碱性。

材料

咖喱粉、酒精、清水、白布条、镊子、小苏打、纸巾、塑料杯、滴管等。

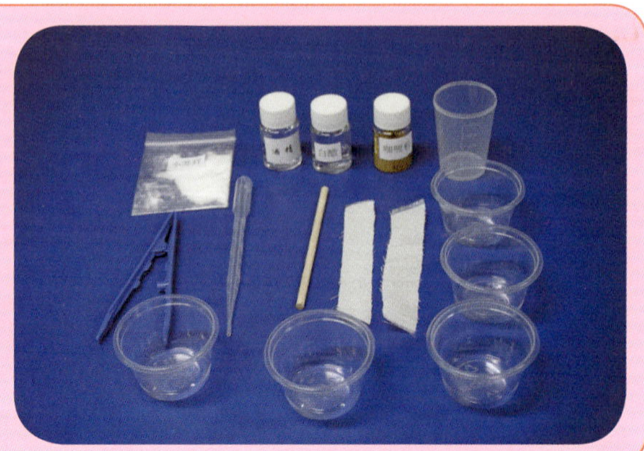

流程

1. 在塑料杯中倒入咖喱粉，并在咖喱粉中倒入酒精。
2. 将咖喱粉和酒精调成糊状。

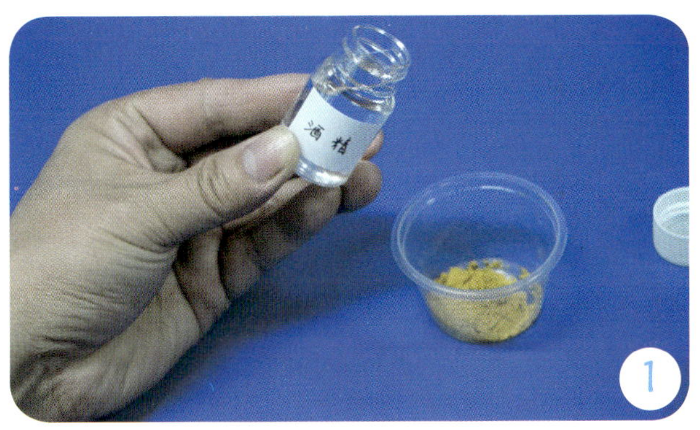

3. 把干净的白布条投入其中浸透，静置一会儿，然后用镊子取出，发现白布已呈黄色。

4. 用清水洗白布表面的咖喱粉。将布条用纸巾吸水后再晾干，就制成了黄色的咖喱粉酸碱指示布条了，它的颜色与pH试纸一样，也是黄色的。

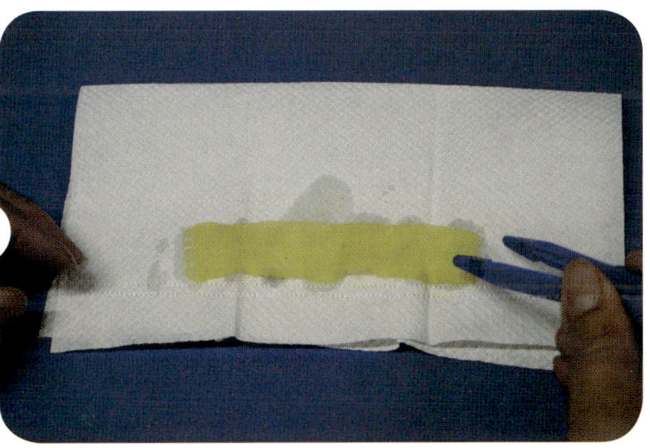

5. 在塑料杯中倒入一些小苏打，并加入少许的水，搅拌制成小苏打溶液。

6. 用滴管将小苏打溶液滴在咖喱粉酸碱指示布条表面，发现布条变成了浅红色，说明咖喱粉酸碱指示布条遇碱性物质变红色。这样的黄色小布条可以检验家里日常用的碱性溶液。

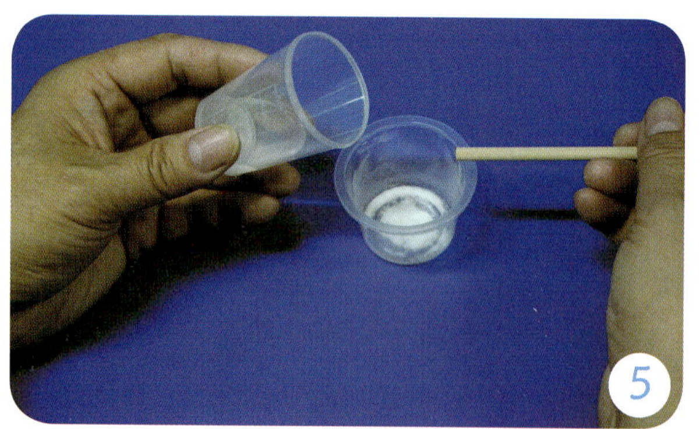
5

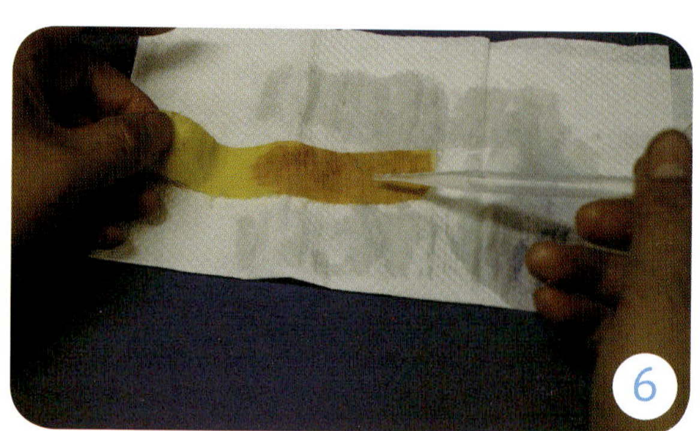
6

拓展

用紫甘蓝制作酸碱指示剂：

①把紫甘蓝切成丁放在容器里，注入沸水，10 分钟后水变成了紫色，滤掉紫甘蓝菜叶，把紫甘蓝水放在烧杯中待用。

②在两只小烧杯中倒入适量清水，在第一个杯中倒入小苏打（碱性溶液），第二个杯中倒入少许白醋（酸性溶液）。当在每个杯中都倒入一些紫色的紫甘蓝水后，杯中原来透明的水开始变色：第一杯（碱性溶液）变成绿色，第二杯（酸性溶液）变成红色。

紫甘蓝水也是一种酸碱指示剂。

第五课 转动的风车

风能利用的历史

我国是世界上利用风能最早的国家之一。汉字“帆”可以在甲骨文字中找到，说明我国利用风能有着悠久的历史。我们利用风力提水、灌溉、舂米、磨面，利用风帆使船舶前进。在宋代，我国就已普遍使用垂直轴风车，并一直沿用至今。

外国对风的利用与我国的情况相似。值得一提的是荷兰风车，常用在莱茵河三角洲湖地和低湿地汲水，也用于锯木和榨油。当蒸汽机出现后，风车的使用才逐渐减少。

风能发电机

在山上、海边、草原，我们常常可以见到一种像纸风车一样的物体，这就是风能发电机。风能让纸风车转动，同样，人们利用风作为动力带动机械装置发电。人们通常在四季风力较多、风能大小比较稳定的地方建发电厂（风速大于4米/秒，但不能超过25米/秒），利用风能进行发电。此外，在同等条件下，海上风能发电厂的产电量是陆地的7倍。

STEM 制作：制作纸风车

科学 知道纸风车的转动原理；

技术 了解制作纸风车的步骤；

工程 观察、制作并测试纸风车；

数学 掌握纸的对角线、等分线及中心点。

目标

1. 通过制作纸风车了解风扇面方向不同，所吹动纸风车的风向不同。
2. 通过制作电动风车了解风扇叶片的角度不同，所吹出的风力大小不同。
3. 通过制作电动风车了解风扇数量不同，风力不同。

材料

卡纸、剪刀、工字钉、双面胶、回形针、吸管、电池盒、电池、电动机、塑料轮胎、尺等。

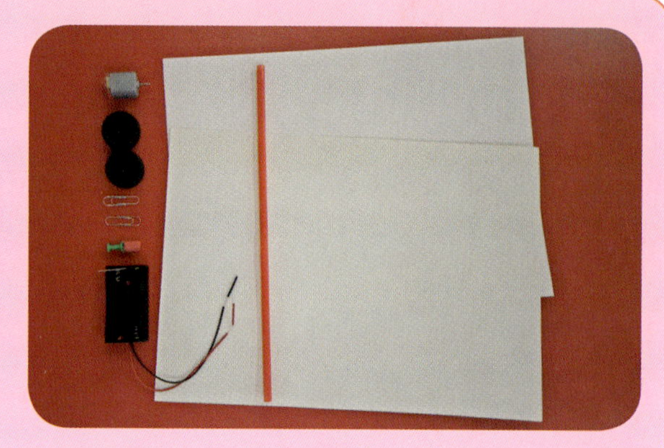

流程

【制作一】制作纸风车

1. 如图所示，对折卡纸，并用剪刀剪下多余部分，形成正方形。
2. 将正方形卡纸沿对角线分别折叠两次，用剪刀沿对角线由外而内剪，不要剪得过于靠近正方形的中心。

①

②

3. 将剪开的四个角按逆时针的顺序拉到中心点，分别用双面胶固定。

4. 用工字钉在风车的中心位置戳一个小孔。

5. 取出吸管，用工字钉在吸管的一端戳一个小孔。

6. 掰开一个回形针，用回形针由风车正面向后穿过中心点，固定在吸管上，不要太紧，保证风车能顺利旋转。完成纸风车的制作后，来回移动风车，观察纸风车的旋转情况。

小贴士

纸风车的转动原理：

纸风车的叶片一高一低形成斜面，风吹来，由于作用力与反作用力的原理，风车就开始转动。

【制作二】探究风扇叶片角度与形成风力大小的关系

1. 在卡纸上画出两个圆，并用剪刀剪下。
2. 用直尺在圆上画出两条相互垂直的直径。

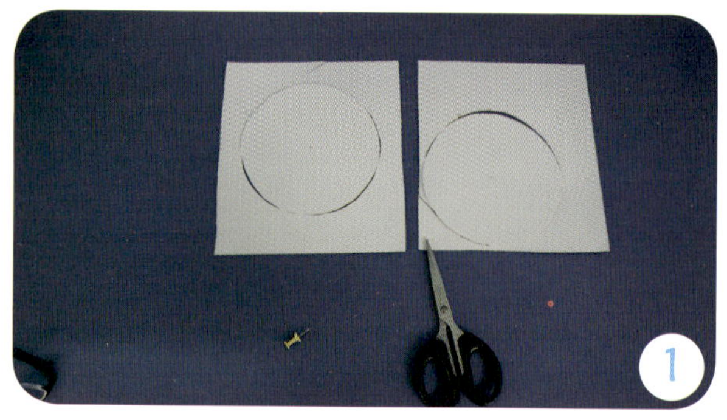
1

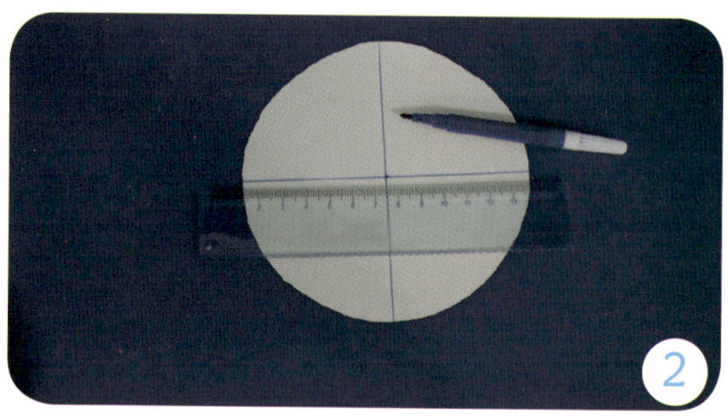
2

3. 用剪刀在半径上剪出四条等长的开口，并向上折出相同的角度。用双面胶将塑料轮胎的正面粘贴于图示位置。
4. 将电池盒与电动机相连接。

3

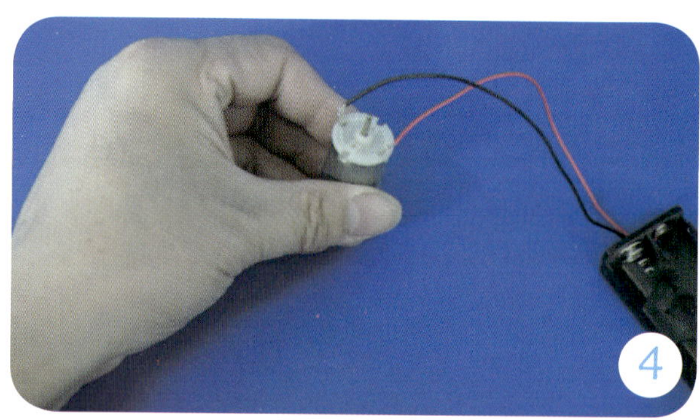
4

5. 将塑料轮胎插入电动机轴上，电池装入电池盒，测试形成风力的大小。
6. 调整风扇的角度，对比研究风扇叶片角度与形成风力大小的关系。

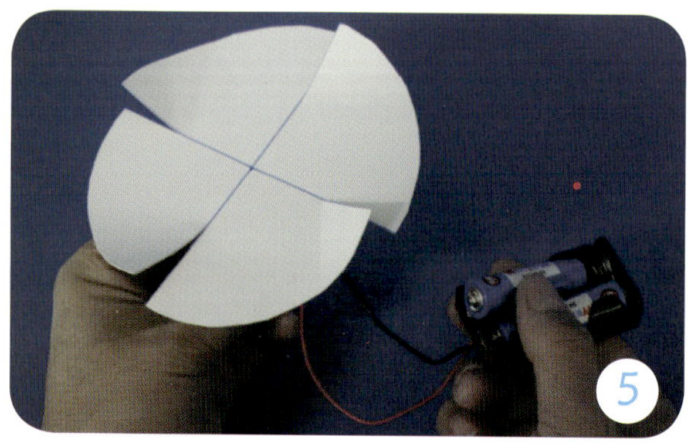
5

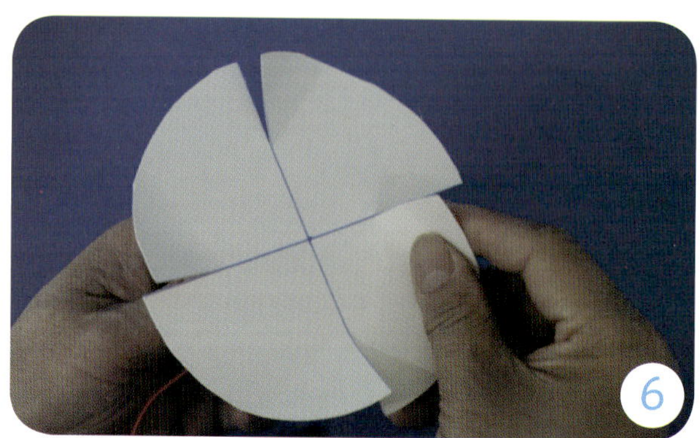
6

【制作三】探究风扇叶片的数量与风力大小的关系

1. 利用文具盒里的三角尺在一个圆纸片上画出三条等分线。

2. 以等分线为参照，用剪刀剪出一个三叶风扇，确保裁剪均匀。
3. 将风扇与电源相连，对比研究叶片数量与风力大小的关系。

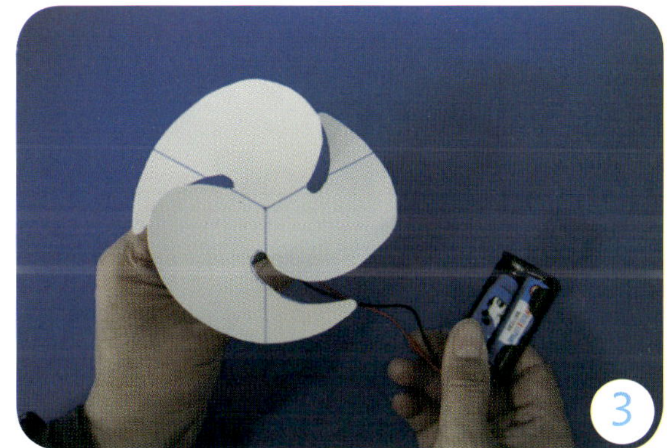

拓展

风能是很洁净的能源，那么，你能不能想办法将风能转化成其他形式的能量呢？

第六课 羽毛球着地时

面对广受欢迎的羽毛球运动项目，当羽毛球着地时，总是球托先着地吗？现在，让我们带着问题一起探索物体运动的科学原理吧！

影响羽毛球着地情况的可能因素包括：力的大小、力的方向、球裙材料、运动环境等。将同学们分组成三组，每组四人，组内四人中两人打羽毛球，第三人观察、拍照，第四人记录实验结果。

探究影响羽毛球着地部位的因素

【实　验】每组任选至少两个影响因素进行探究。每探究一个影响因素绘制一张表格，每个影响因素做五次实验，将实验结果记录在表格中。

【拍照、小视频】略

【结　论】在影响羽毛球着地时的因素中，只改变其中一个因素而其他均相同时，总是球托先着地。

为什么羽毛球着地都是球托先着地

观察羽毛球球托部分和羽毛球羽毛部分，羽毛球的两部分有哪些不同？我们可以发现这两部分的材料不同、形状不同。

分析运动学原理可知：下落过程中物体会旋转，同时受到空气阻力。因球托与球裙材料、形状不同，所以在空气中受到阻力不同，球裙与空气接触面积大，所受阻力大，而球托与空气接触面积小，所受阻力小，故先着地。

哪些物体着地情况类似羽毛球着地

生活中有些物体，如奶油蛋糕、降落伞等物体着地时类似羽毛球着地。奶油蛋糕中的奶油和蛋糕也是两种材料、两种形状。当蛋糕滑落时刻，蛋糕部分的

重心已经在桌外，跌落过程会旋转，奶油部分受到阻力小，所以奶油比蛋糕先着地。西方有俚语说：“蛋糕落地，总是有奶油的一面朝下。”那降落伞呢？一定是人比降落伞先着地。原因是跳伞过程中，降落伞与空气接触面大，所受阻力较大，下降速度慢，后着地。

普通物体着地，若所受阻力小，则着地快。若所受阻力大，则着地慢。若一物体由两部分组成，则所受阻力小的部分，着地快；所受阻力大的部分，着地慢。

但当此类物体在运动中受到外力，则会改变着地方式。例如：用力往地上摔羽毛球的掉落过程中，可能是球裙先着地；运动的物体被绊到，可能会改变运动轨迹和着地方式。

STEM 实践：绘制、制作羽毛球

科学 知道羽毛球着地时，球托比球裙形状小、相对所受到的阻力小，球托先着地；

技术 用塑料瓶、乒乓球、泡沫塑料套制作一个羽毛球；

工程 制作羽毛球；

数学 了解羽毛球三视图的画法。

目标

1. 以羽毛球着地时为研究点，训练同学们质疑、思考、假设、验证的思维过程。
2. 分别用简笔画（训练同学们文字描述）、三视图（指导规范的画图）两种方法，描绘羽毛球的外形比较各自优缺点。
3. 选用多种材料、多种方法（割、填、旋、扎），完成羽毛球的制作，观测整体与局部的表现。

活动一：简笔画绘制羽毛球

流程

【绘 制】通过看简笔画图解，学习绘制羽毛球。

【写步骤】对照简笔画图解，归纳绘图步骤。

画扁方块

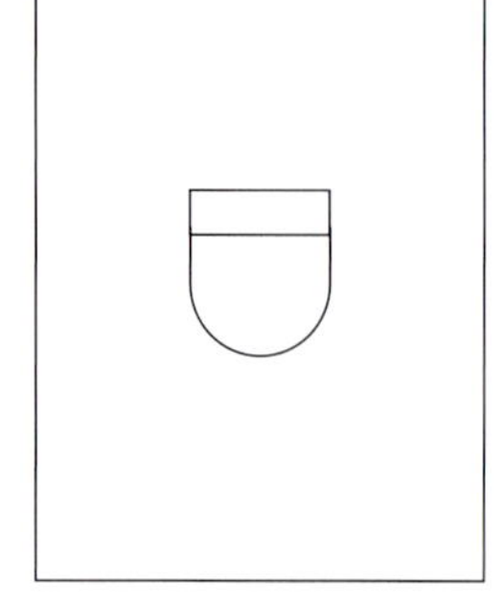
在扁方块下画一圆底

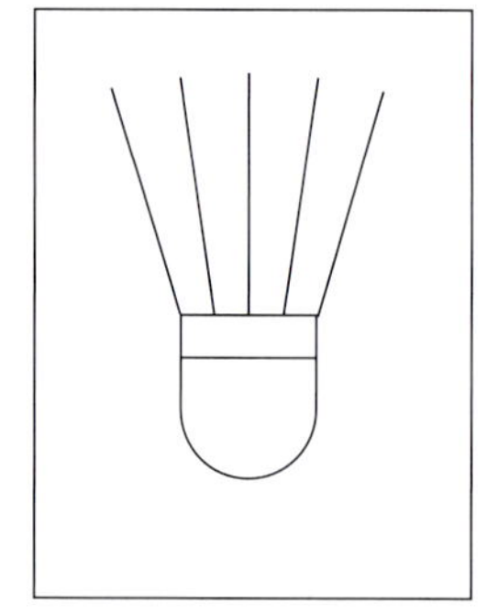
在扁方块上画五条射线

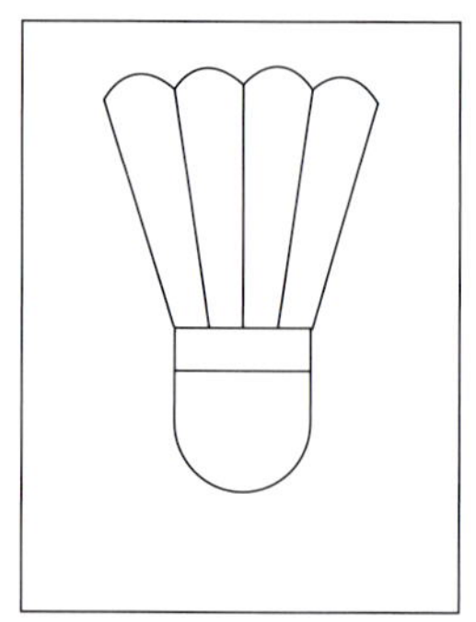
再画4个向下的圆括号

活动二：制作羽毛球

材料

乒乓球、工字钉、剪刀、空饮料瓶、网状泡沫塑料套、热熔胶、蜡烛、彩泥、双面胶等。

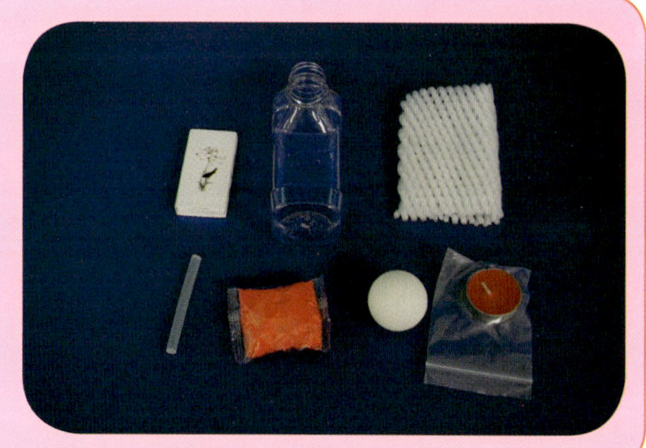

流程

1. 用工字钉在乒乓球上开出一个小孔。

2. 如图所示，用剪刀插入小孔中，剪出一个开口，开口大小比空饮料瓶瓶口稍大。

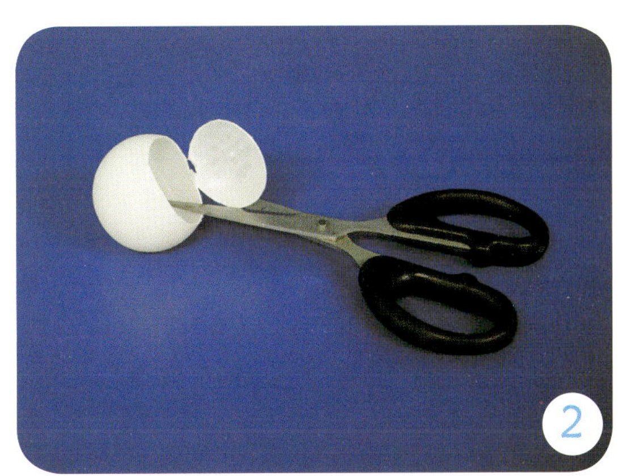

3. 如图所示，用剪刀剪下饮料瓶瓶口。

4. 将饮料瓶的瓶口塞入乒乓球中。

5. 点燃蜡烛加热热熔胶，用热熔胶在乒乓球内部固定乒乓球与瓶口的连接处。

6. 用双面胶在乒乓球与瓶口的外部连接处缠绕一圈。

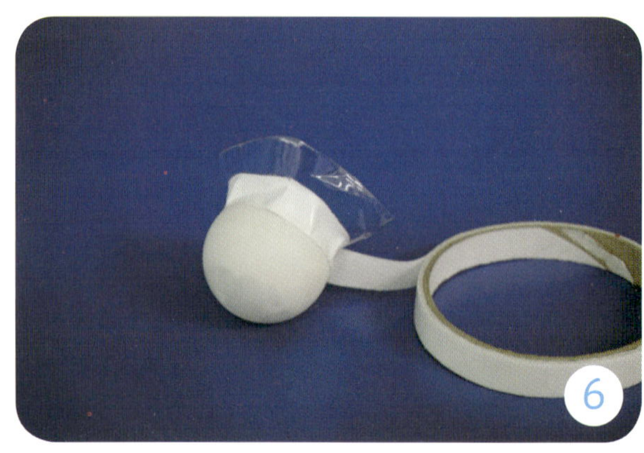

7. 粘贴网状泡沫塑料套于乒乓球的外部，并用剪刀剪去网状泡沫塑料套多余的部分。

8. 用剪刀将网状泡沫塑料套剪成条状，模拟羽毛球的羽毛。

9. 在乒乓球内加入适量的彩泥进行配重，完成羽毛球的制作。改变羽毛球内部的配重重量，测试羽毛球在空气中的运动情况。

拓展

用制作的羽毛球进行一场单打比赛。基本规则：双方中分数先达 21 分者胜，3 局 2 胜。每局双方打到 20 平后，一方领先 2 分即算该局获胜；若双方打成 29 平后，率先得到第 30 分的即算该局取胜。

第七课　无线遥控车

基于英国科学家麦克斯韦的“电磁波传播”理论的无线电通信技术，最早应用于航海，人们使用摩尔斯电码实现陆地与海上的通信。

目前，基于无线电通信技术的无线遥控系统在军事、生活、医疗等领域应用广泛。小到儿童的玩具，大到巡航战斗机，都载有无线遥控系统。现代无线遥控系统的控制作用距离可以是几米，也可以是上万千米。

什么是无线遥控系统

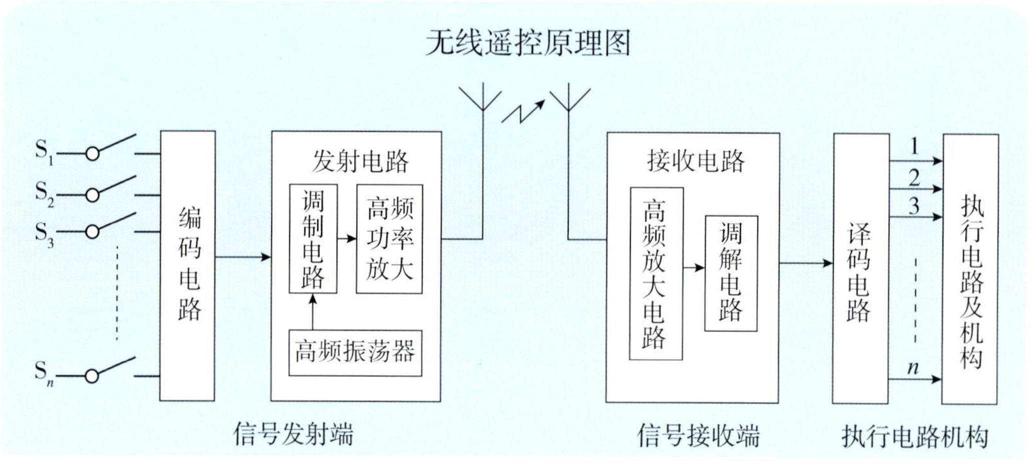

无线遥控系统主要由发射机、接收机及执行机三部分组成。发射机包括编码电路和发射电路，接收机包括接收天线、接收电路和解调电路，执行机包括译码电路和执行电路。

接收天线将无线电波转换成微弱的电信号，经接收电路内高频放大电路选择和放大后，再经解调，从载波中卸下指令信号。卸下的各种指令信号混杂在一起，需先使用译码电路进行译码，再分别传送至相应的执行电路及机构中。执行电路则将指令信号放大，使之具有一定的功率以驱动执行机构动作，实现对被控物体的控制。

执行机构是根据控制指令产生动作的装置，如电磁铁、电机、电磁阀等。

什么是编码电路

编码是指在发送端为达到预定的目的，将原始信号按一定规则进行处理的过程。也就是信息从一种形式或格式转化为另一种形式的过程。

在无线电领域，我们通常将每秒的周波数称为频率。如频率为 1000 Hz 的音频信号每秒便有 1000 个正弦波的周波。编码电路产生的指令信号都是频率较低的电信号，一般无法直接通过天线传送到遥控目标上去。因此，需要通过调制将其搭载在高频载波上才能由天线发送出去。

什么是调制

调制，指对信号源的信息进行处理，使其变为适合于信道传输形式的过程，是通过改变高频载波（即消息的载体）信号的幅度、相位或者频率，使其随着基带信号幅度的变化而变化来实现的。

什么是解调

解调是调制的逆过程，指将收到的信号还原成最初的形式，一般通过还原信号的频率、幅度及其他性质实现。

我们要做的无线遥控车是什么样的

我们要制作的无线遥控车，包含“前进”和“后退”两个功能，最大遥控距离为 4 ~ 5 米。同频率的无线遥控车会互相干扰，不能在一起同时使用。小车接收到多个相同频率的信号就会乱转。

STEM 实践：制作无线遥控车

科学 了解无线遥控系统工作原理；

技术 了解无线遥控车的组装步骤；

工程 能够组装并测试无线遥控车；

数学 测量无线遥控车的遥控距离。

目标

1. 能够组装小车。
2. 能够使用遥控器遥控小车。
3. 了解遥控原理。

材料

电路板、电机、电机固定夹、栅格板、车轮、车轴、接线器、电池盒、窗板、螺丝、轴座架、天线等。

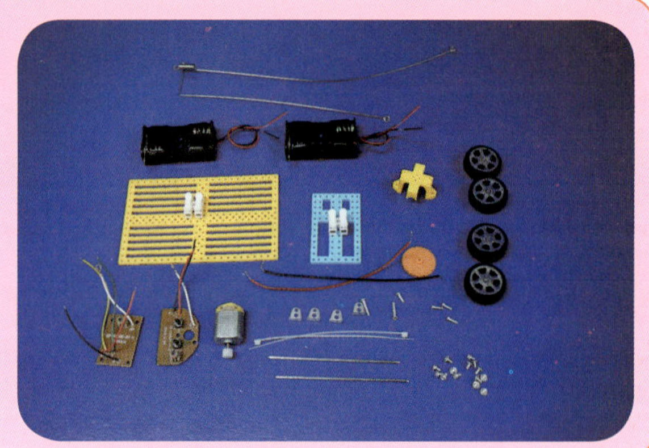

流程

1. 参照图 1，把接收电路板上的绿线和黄线分别接到电机上，接线时请确保电路板无电。

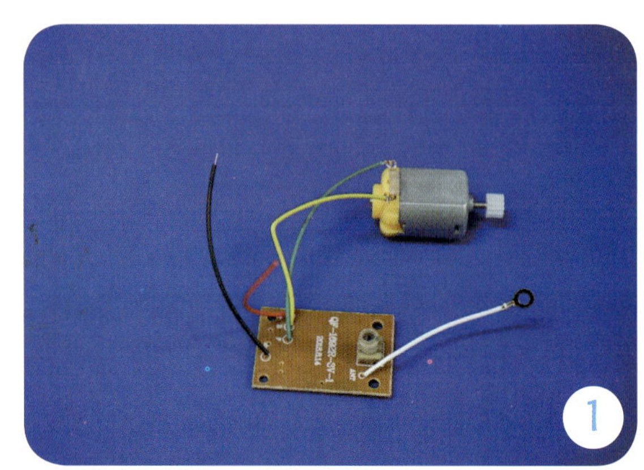
1

2. 参照图2孔位，用4 mm粗纹螺丝把4个轴座架安装到栅格板的四个角，并把车轮组件安装好，车轴从轴架座的中间孔穿过；再用电机固定夹和7 mm螺丝把电机安装到车架上。

3. 参照图3，首先用一颗4 mm螺丝把电路板固定在车架上，然后把电路板上的红黑线分别卡入接线器的两个口；然后用一颗12 mm螺丝把白色的接线器固定在车架上；紧接着把电池盒的输出线卡入接线器的另一端，红线对红线，黑线对黑线；最后用两颗4 mm螺丝把电池盒固定在车架上。

2

3

4. 参照图4孔位，用一颗4 mm螺丝把天线安装好，车子组装完成。

5. 参照图5孔位，首先用一颗4 mm螺丝把遥控电路板安装到窗板上；然后用一颗4 mm螺丝把天线安装在窗板右侧；紧接着用一颗12 mm螺丝把接线器安装在窗板左侧；最后把遥控电路板的红、黑线卡入接线器。

4

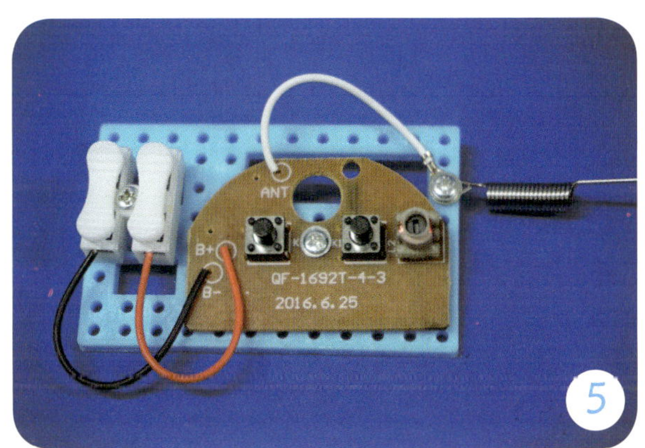

5

6. 参照图 6，用两颗 4 mm 螺丝把电池盒安装在遥控电路板的背面，另外把电池盒的输出线卡入白色的接线器，红线对红线，黑线对黑线卡入。

7. 遥控车组装完成，安装电池，闭合开关，调试遥控车吧！

拓展

无线遥控车我们已经完成，下一步你可以尝试使用蓝牙或者 APP 来控制小车。

第八课　激光红外报警器

激光是指激发态原子受激辐射的光。被激发出的光子队列光学性质相同，具有很高的能量，激光也因此被称为“最快的刀”“最准的尺”“最亮的光”。

早在1917年，爱因斯坦就提出了“受激辐射”的理论。43年之后，科学家们经过不断的尝试，激光器问世。1964年，著名物理学家钱学森正式将LASER（“通过辐射受激发射的光放大”的英文缩写）翻译为“激光”。

激光报警器是激光的一个应用方面，主要用于探测敌方激光武器、激光制导武器等被动侦察装备，通常由扫描天线、激光监别器、放大器、微处理机、指令控制器、报警显示器等组成。

激光红外报警器是如何工作的

报警器光线发射端所使用的激光红外线的光束线是直线型且不散光，能够精准定位照射。而光感控制端的光敏电阻能根据是否被红外线激光照射改变阻值。当红外线照射到光敏电阻时，其阻值很小，电路中电流很大；反之，红外线激光被遮挡，光敏电阻阻值增大，电流减小。由此得出的两个大小不同的电流值可以控制三极管电路，从而控制报警器工作。

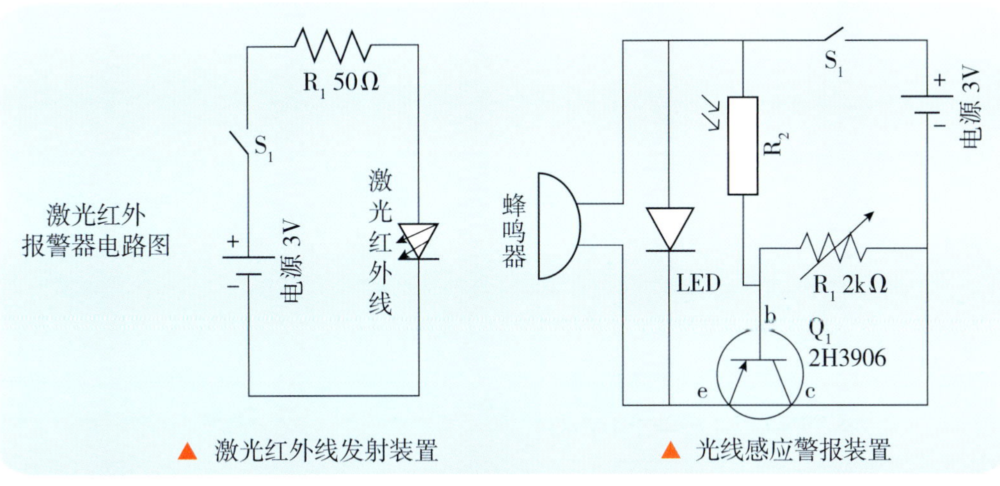

▲ 激光红外线发射装置　▲ 光线感应警报装置

如何保护三极管不因电流过大而损坏

我们为控制极 b 极加上电阻以限制电流。在报警器的电路中，“+”极是光敏电阻，“-”极是阻值可调的电阻，它们都可以用来缩小流经 b 极的电流。

我们要做的激光红外报警器是怎样的

在此模型中，我们使用 PNP 型三极管来控制电路。当激光一直照射光敏电阻时，光敏电阻为三极管 b 极提供了一股“+”电流，此时 e 极到 c 极是不导通状态，LED 灯与蜂鸣器都不工作。而当激光束被遮挡，光敏电阻阻值变大，此时 b 极“-”电流大于“+”电流，导致 e 极到 c 极被导通，LED 灯和蜂鸣器开始工作。在这个三极管电路中，b 极相当于一个开关，控制着电流的方向。

如何使用激光红外报警器

1. 单直线对射布线

将红外线对准光感警报器的光敏电阻即可。

2. 多直线折射布线

利用小镜子作为红外线的反射点，经过多次反射将其由红外线发射点最终折射到光敏电阻上。使用该布线方法将产生多条激光红外线。

STEM 实践：制作激光红外报警器

科学 理解激光红外报警器工作原理；

技术 学会激光红外报警器的组装；

工程 能够组装激光红外报警器；

数学 能计算报警的距离。

目标

1. 能够组装激光报警器。
2. 能够了解激光报警器原理。
3. 能够计算并优化所需要用的报警距离。

材料

窗板、L 型角码、直杆、接线器、蜂鸣器、发光二极管、三极管、可调电阻、光敏电阻、电池盒、电池、栅栏式接线端子、激光头、螺丝、双面胶等。

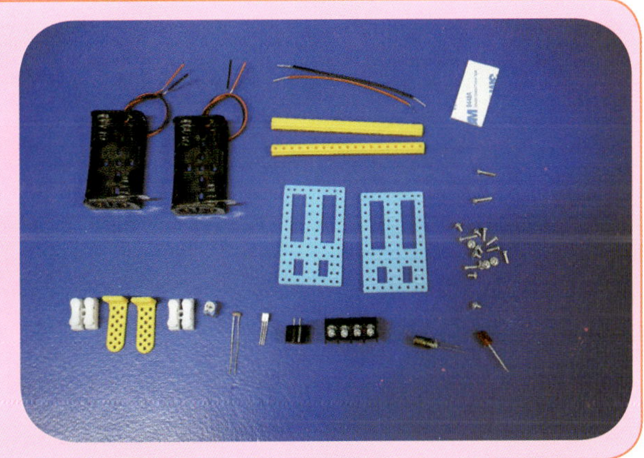

流程

1. 首先参照图 1，用 4 mm 粗纹螺丝把 L 型角码装到窗板上，接着把短直杆用粗纹螺丝装到 L 型角码上，并把接线器用 10 mm 螺丝固定在直杆顶端，螺丝不需要拧太紧，因为装成成品后要做上下旋转调节。

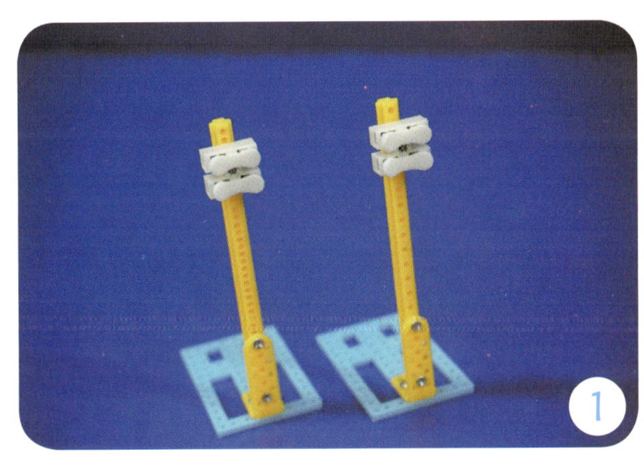
1

2. 仔细观察电路接线图，安装电子元器件及接线请参考此图。注意看可调节电阻的形状，找出 3 个引脚的位置。可调电阻只能接 1 和 2 引脚，或 2 和 3 引脚，否则电阻无法工作。

3. 参照图 3 与“电路接线图”，把线路及元器件装好。注意三极管必须字母面朝上，可调电阻三个引脚只接两个，另一个引脚悬空。蜂鸣器与发光二极管需要分正、负极，长引脚接正极，短引脚接负极，蜂鸣器的贴纸请在组装完成后移除。

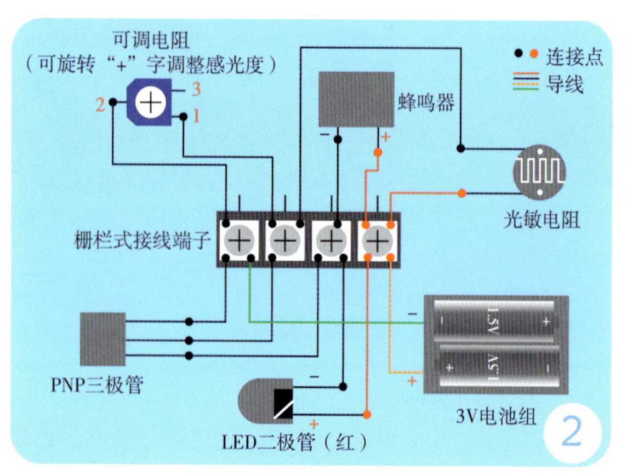

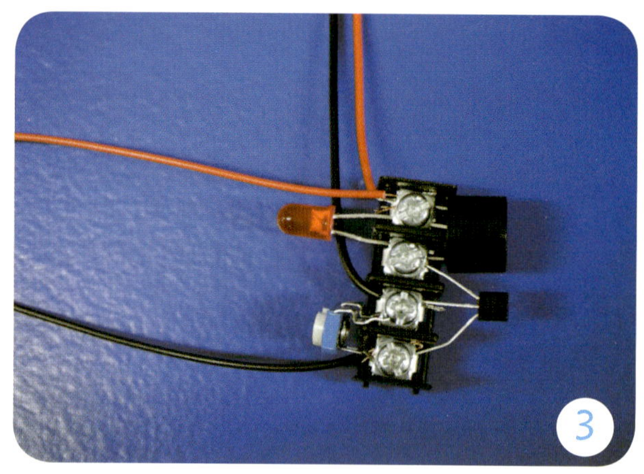

4. 参考图 4，把电池盒用 4 mm 粗纹螺丝装到窗板上，然后剪一小片双面胶粘到直杆上，接着把接线端子粘到直杆的双面胶上，然后把红、黑线卡入接线器。

5. 参照图 5，把光敏电阻卡入接线器（不需要分正负极），使电阻与直杆平行（有利于之后对接）。报警器端组装完成。

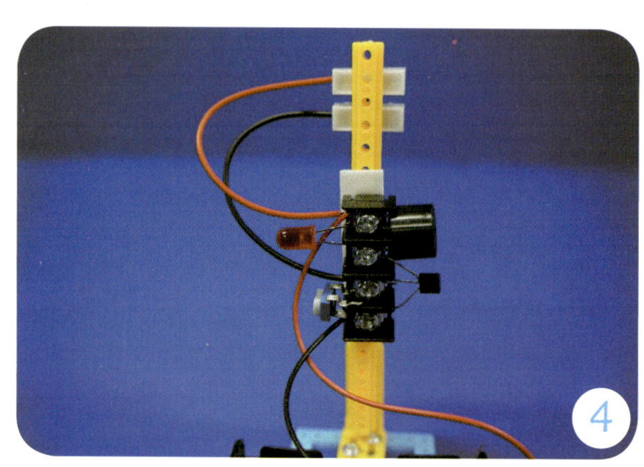

6. 把电池盒用4mm粗纹螺丝装到窗板上，然后把电池盒输出线卡入接线器。

7. 把激光头卡入接线器，激光头长引脚卡入红线口，短引脚卡入黑线口。红外线发生端组装完成。

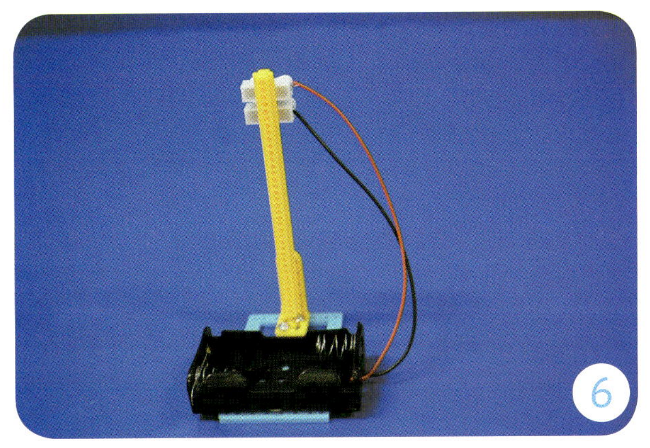

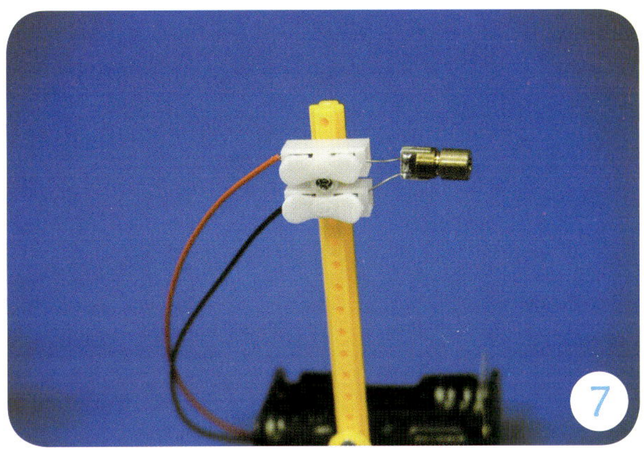

8. 分别在报警端和发射端安装电池，打开电池盒上的开关，激光束必须射在光敏电阻上，可以通过上下微调接线器将激光红外线对准光敏电阻。注意，接通电源后蜂鸣器默认响起，发光二极管也会亮起，需要把激光对准光敏电阻后，蜂鸣器和发光二极管才停止工作，此时为报警器的正常工作状态。如果激光对准后还是一直响，请用螺丝刀调整可调电阻，电阻白色圆圈可转动。如果接通后蜂鸣器不响，请检查元器件是否安装正确。

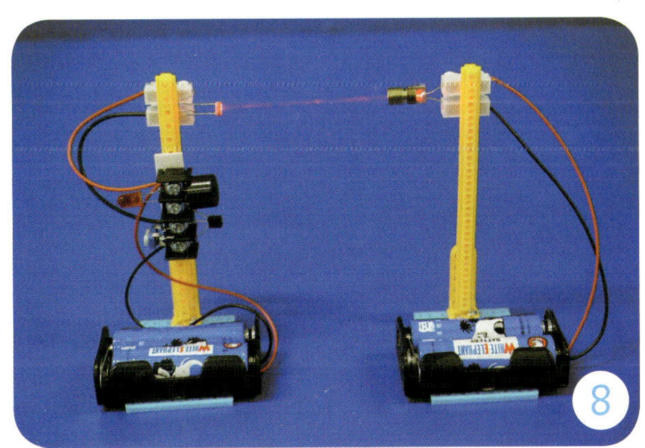

拓展

你可以尝试一下，看看红外激光报警器有没有距离的限制。

CONTENT

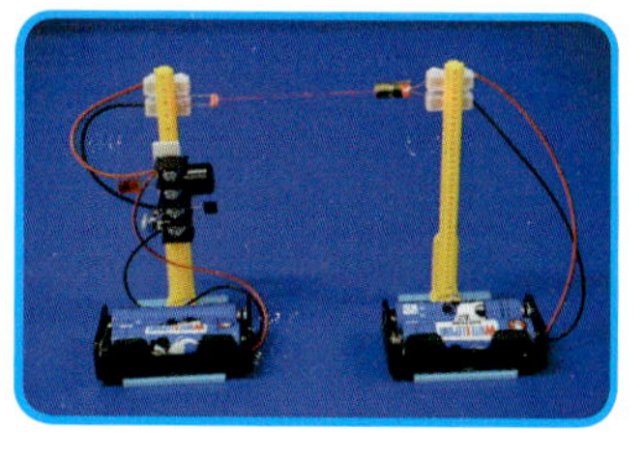

Lesson 1 Compass

As we know, compass is one of the four great inventions in ancient China, which can also be called Sinan. Compass can identify the direction of south and north by pointing to them respectively, which is helpful in our life.

Then, do you know why compass can identify the direction of south and north? A compass is a magnet. It has its own S pole and N pole. The Earth has two magnetic poles too. Its magnetic field is similar to that of a bar magnet.

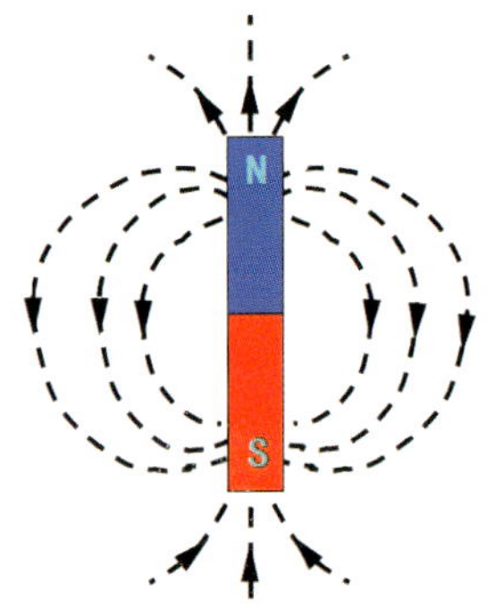

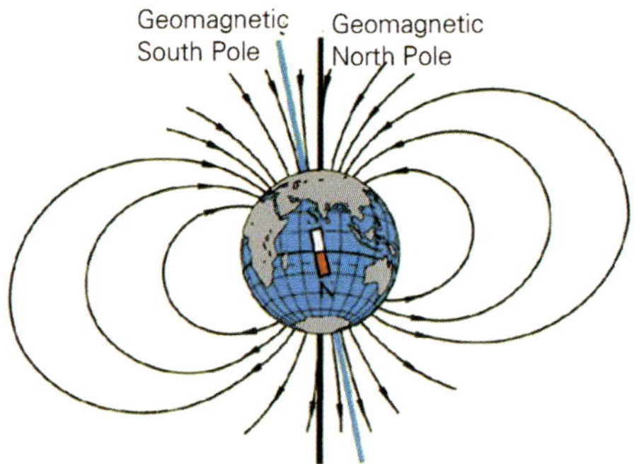

We all know that the same poles repel each other (N–N or S–S), while the opposite magnetic poles attract each other (N–S or S–N). Therefore, under the influence of the Earth's magnetic field, the N pole of the compass will be attracted by the S pole of Earth, and the S pole of compass will be attracted by the N pole of Earth.

The small magnetic needle will therefore align with the magnetic field lines of the planet. But we should notice that the magnetic south pole is Earth's geographical north pole. Vice versa. In other words, the two

geographical poles of Earth are opposite to those of terrestrial magnetism.

In fact, there is still a small angle between the two poles of terrestrial magnetism and of geography, usually we call it magnetic declination. The degree of this angle varies in different places. In China it is usually 2° ~6° .

Well, after this introduction to the working principles of compass, do you think it's possible to make your own compass?

STEM Practice: Making a Compass

Science	Understand magnetism and the basic working principle of magnets;
Technology	Be able to magnetize other objects by rubbing them with magnets;
Engineering	Learn to make a simple compass;
Mathematics	Understand the use of compass and visualize the lines and planes in a magnetic field.

Objectives

1. To understand the magnetic field of the Earth.
2. To understand the interaction between different magnetic poles (N/S) and the direction the compass points to.
3. To understand what are magnetization and demagnetization.
4. To learn to make a usable compass.

Materials

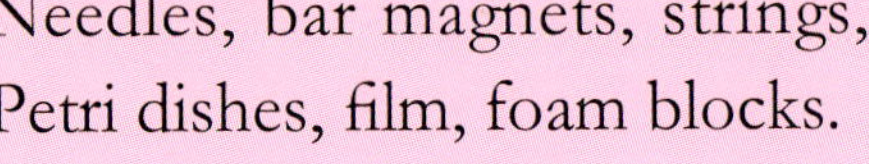
Needles, bar magnets, strings,
Petri dishes, film, foam blocks.

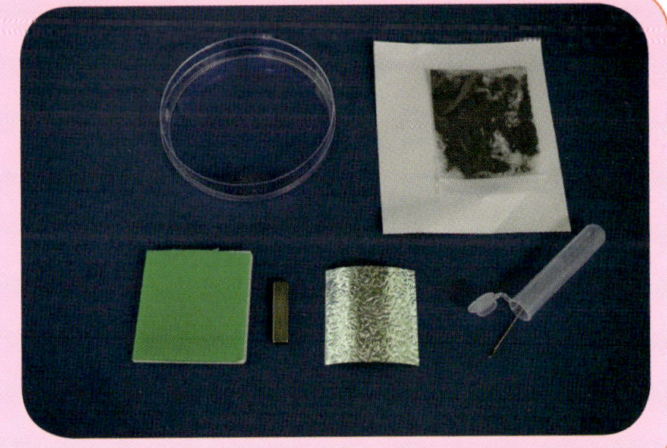

Process

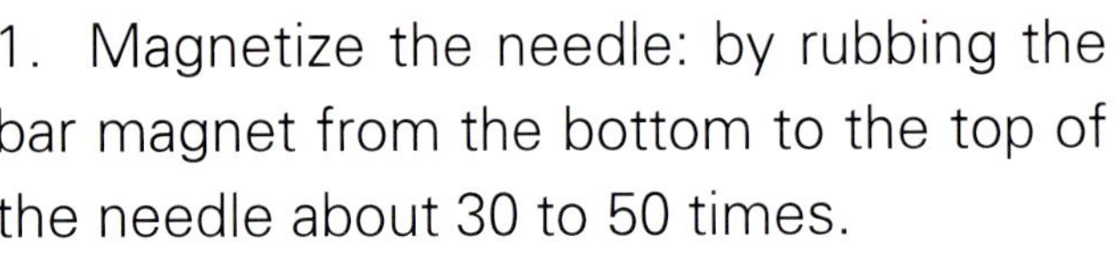
1. Magnetize the needle: by rubbing the bar magnet from the bottom to the top of the needle about 30 to 50 times.

2. Hang the needle up and the pinpoint will point the South when it is still. Make sure you keep the bar magnet far away enough.

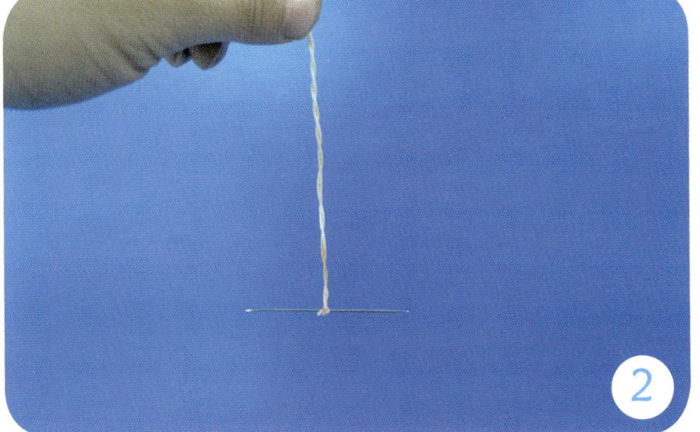

3. You can also put the magnetized needle on the foam block, and put the block in water in the Petri dish. No matter how you place it, the pinpoint will always point the South. If the foam piece is too big to fit in, you may cut it into any size that fits the Petri dish.

4. Put the magnetized needle on the film and then put them in water in the Petri dish. The pinpoint will point the South, even if you rotate the dish.

Extension

Put some iron powder into a sealable bag, then hold a magnet on the bag. Observe the movement and distribution of iron powder. Try to explain the scientific principles related.

Lesson 2 Civil Engineering

Infrastructure is a basic system to serve for an entire country, which sustains the function of transportation and economy, including roads, bridges, tunnels, sewers, power grids, water supply and communication (including Internet), etc.

Bridges are an important part of our infrastructure. Bridges are the works of many engineers and construction workers, and they're not simple works at all! Though the appearance of a bridge is important, much more importance should be attached to its safety in use. For several months, a bridge project must be designed and tested. So engineers can plan, design, test, simulate real situations, and plan again until they can be sure that the project will work.

Bridges are massive constructions. Sometimes they can be several kilometers in length and a few hundreds of meters in height. They have thousands of components made of steel and concrete. On the bridge, there may be thousands of tons of cars, trucks, buses and trains running. The bridge itself may be subject to many different forces, such as the gravity, compression and tension. This is why engineers must use their knowledge of physics to calculate and deal with these problems.

The huge weight of a bridge means it is constantly being pulled down by gravity. This force will affect all the components, creating compression and tension.

Compression is a force that squishes the materials inward. Some objects shrink when compressed—like bread. Harder objects can sustain certain level of compression, but if it's too strong, they will break! When something like this

happens, it usually happens in unpredictable ways, as it's hard to know exactly where the weak points are.

In comparison, tension is a force in the opposite direction—it stretches outward. Some objects extend when compressed—like balloons. Many materials can resist some degrees of stretching, and in fact, moderate tension can make materials stronger! Have you ever seen an acrobat do tightrope walking? Well, that would not be possible if the rope was not tight (with tension applied to it). Without tension, the rope and the poor acrobat would both fall! However, too much tension can also cause the material to rip itself apart. We need to be aware of the tension and compression forces happening on all parts of our bridge. We need to balance them and control them in a safe way... How can we do this?

For many years, engineers has been using a truss structure to solve the problem, which is very safe and effective. If you look closely at a bridge—take the Golden Gate Bridge as an example—you will find many shapes, especially triangles. Triangles are known as "the strongest shapes", because they are good at balancing forces of tension and compression.

What we can learn:

The Forces

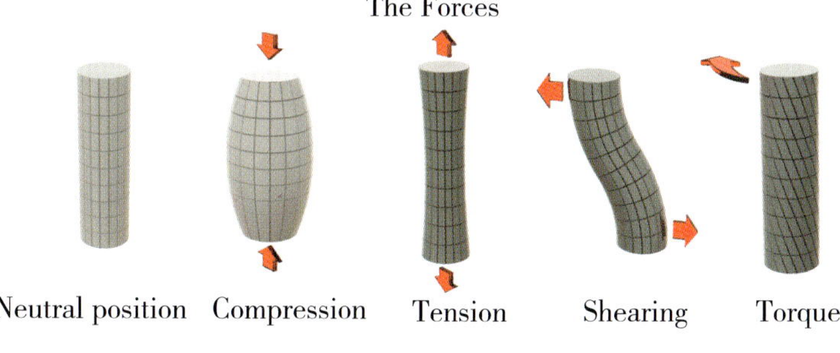

Truss is a type of structure that combines five or more triangle units to make the construction (a bridge or a roof, for example) a whole single object. This is an effective way to balance the combination of forces acting on the objects, such as the gravity, the tension and compression.

The architects and engineers must also consider many other problems, such as snow storms, huge winds, earthquakes and even the traffic.

If any of these forces get too strong even on a single point, the entire bridge could collapse! That's why it's important to spend a long time testing, designing, and fixing the problems that can be predicted. You will experience this by yourself as you try to build your own bridge. Notice where the problems are, then make changes to fix the issues. Step by step, you will be able to have a great final product!

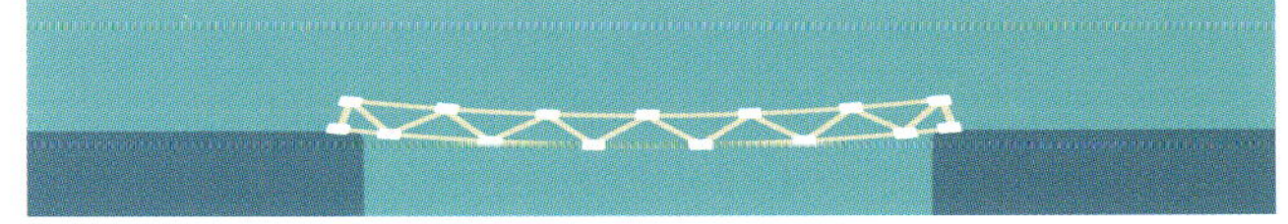

A simple drawing of what a truss bridge can look like

STEM Practice: Building a Truss Bridge

Science	Deal with the forces applied to it to build something;
Technology	Building infrastructure is a kind of technology, which depend on machines and materials;
Engineering	Engineering is more than building. It's the whole process of designing and making decisions;
Mathematics	Understand the geometric shape of the bridge and do calculations about the forces on it for safety.

Objectives

1. To understand the concept of force and its application in engineering.
2. To know the differences among tension, compression, shear and torsion.
3. To know that the safety, stability and durability of a project test on the shape of it.

Materials

Wooden sticks of different sizes (10 cm, 15 cm, 20 cm), styrofoam spheres, flat craft sticks, heavy objects for testing.

Process

1. Build a basic triangle structure by joining the sticks to the styrofoam spheres. Don't pierce them too hard in case of damaging them.

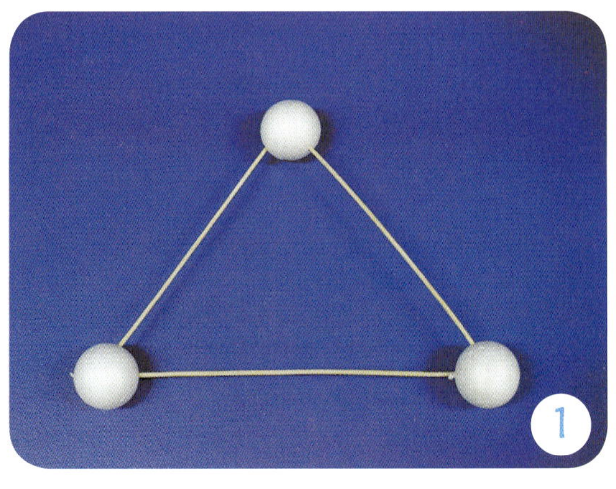

2. You probably need to make more pieces of the same structure you build to make your frame stand up. Pay attention to the angles between the sticks.

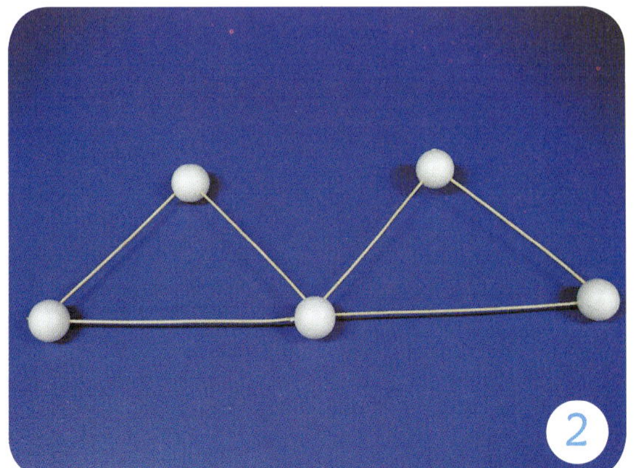

3. Keep building! Join more and more structures together.
4. Insert the short sticks vertically at one side of the bigger structure. Pay attention to the inserting angles.

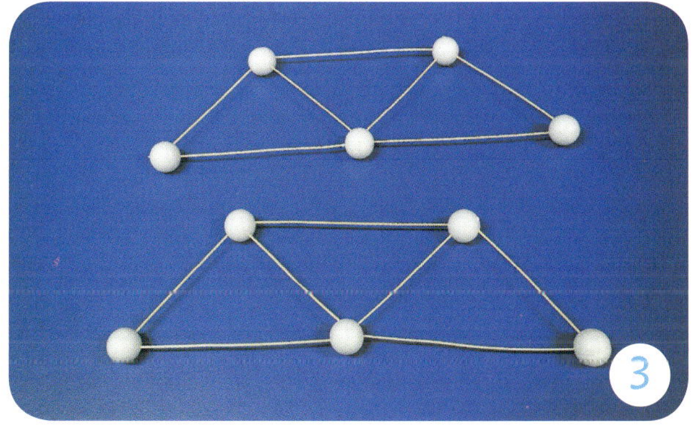

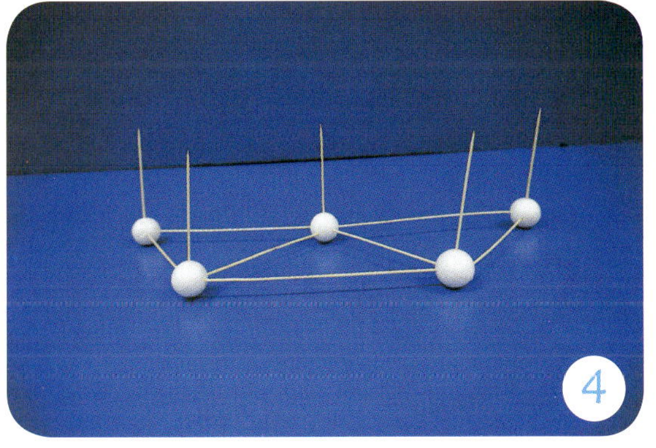

5. Combine the structures together to finish building the frame of the bridge. Observe the points that may cause collapse. Can you see how the tension and compression may cause some problems and change the shape of the bridge? Find them out and fix the issues.
6. Cover the bottom of your frame to finish the building of your bridge. Once you have completed your bridge, test it by putting some weight on it. Imagine a very heavy train is passing on it. Will the bridge break on a single point? See what you can do to avoid that.

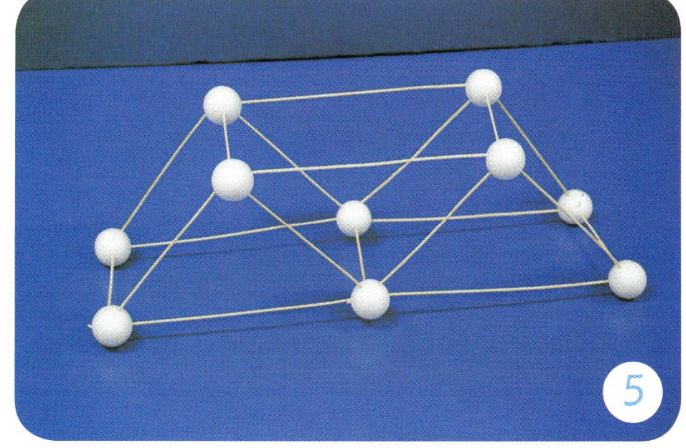

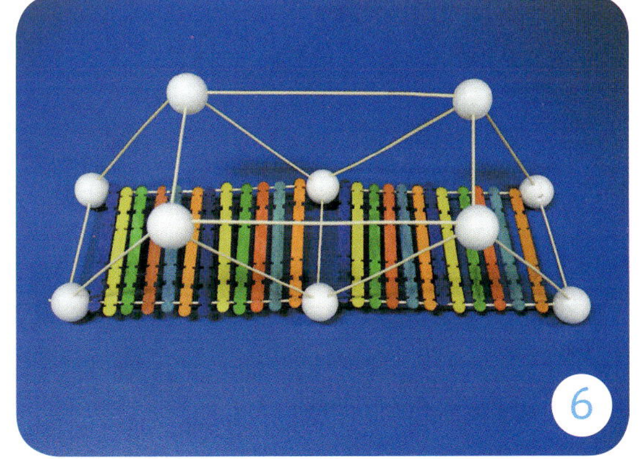

7. Lengthen the bridge and think: what should you do to support the bridge? Will you support it only on the two ends? Can you build it over a gap between two tables? Or is there any other support pillar needed below it ?

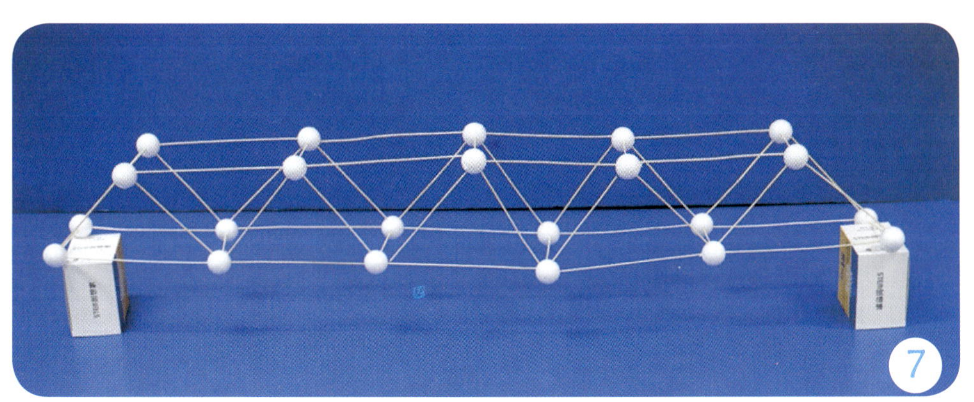

Extension

Remember you can cut the sticks short—that can help you out in some tricky situations. You can make equilateral triangles, isosceles triangles and oblique triangles to set up different frame shapes.

If the styrofoam spheres get damaged because of over using, it's better to just replace them!

Lesson 3 Humidity Sensor

In a crowded public place, to ensure a comfortable and suitable environment for the public and electronic equipments, engineers often set up humidity sensors in the vetilation systems. These sensors can help staffs acquire real–time environmental parameters. In our lives, humidity sensors can be found in areas of meteorological observation, plant cultivation, cultural relics protecting and paper making.

What is a humidity sensor?

So, how can scientists use a simple device to visualize the intangible humidity conditions? In a nutshell, humidity sensors amplify the electrical signals flowing in humid objects through audions. By using resistors and transistors in the circuits, we can convert the degree of humidity into control signals to an LED or a buzzer.

What is the difference between PNP and NPN?

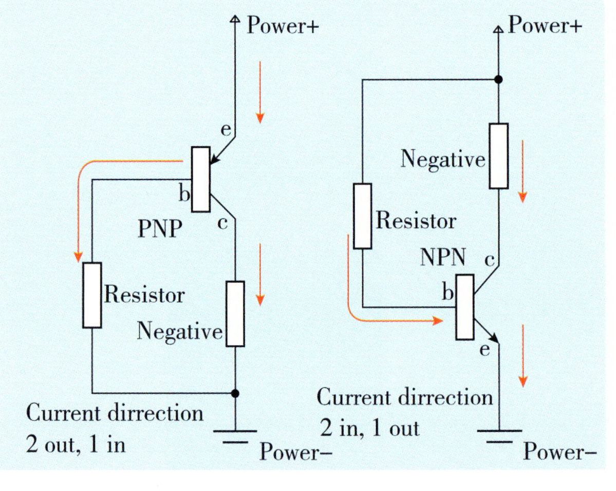

Picture 1

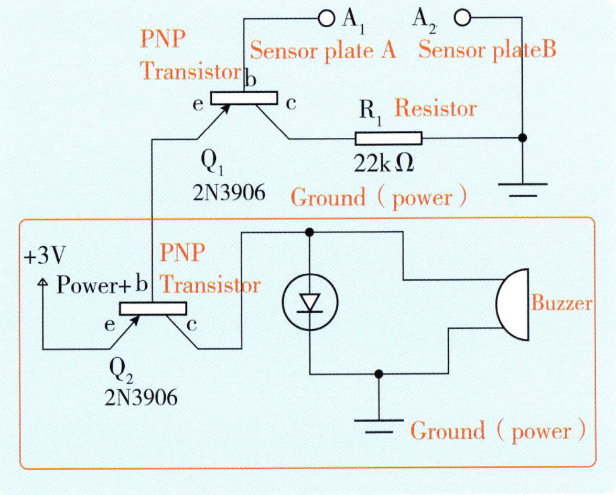

Picture 2

Scientists usually make two PN Junctions closely on a semiconduction substrate, dividing the substrate into three parts. The central part is called the base region, the others are the emitter region and the collector region. There are two possible ways to make arrangements: PNP and NPN.

We can see a difference in current direction between a PNP triode and an NPN triode in Picture 1. The triode has three poles: e—emitter, b—base, and c—collector. If the transistor is used as a switch, taking the PNP arrangement as an example, the e pole can be conducted to the c pole only by connecting the positive pole of the power source with the b pole. On the contrary, if the b pole has no connection or doesn't connect with the positive pole of the power source, the access between e pole and c pole would be closed. In this situation, a resistance will be needed at b pole to limit the current running through it. If the current was higher than the rated current between b pole and c pole, the transistor would be heated–up rapidly, which would destroy it.

We are going to make a circuit based on the diagram in Picture 2, which uses two PNP units to amplify the signal of the sensor. The "control center" of this circuit is highlighted by a rounded rectangle. When the b pole of Q2 is connected to the c pole of Q1, the access between the e pole and c pole of Q2 will be opened, making the LED light and the buzzer ring.

Outside the solid rounded rectangle is the signal–amplification part of the circuit. The audion at Q1 amplifies the signal of A1, connecting the e pole to c pole of Q1 then to ground, while gaining access from b pole of Q2 to c pole of Q1. If there is no signal from A1, then the access between e pole to c pole of Q1 will be closed, and Q2 will remain in a non–conducting state.

In fact, there is also a hidden test circuit in this diagram. If we connect the b pole of Q1 with A1, and A2 with ground, then by simply connecting A1 to A2, it will form a closed circuit. Therefore, when using the humidity sensor, an unmeasured resistor will be required to insulate A1 and A2, which could be, for example, a part of the human body, a piece of dry or humid paper, or a sample of soil. Generally,

the resistance of these conductors are quite high.

How does the humidity sensor work?

Hold A1 and A2 together to make sure they are connected. Then there will be current passing through Q1 triode, and the signal from A1 will be amplified, so that the e pole and c pole of Q1 are connected. Similarly, Q2 will amplify the signal of Q1 once again, making the e pole and c pole of Q2 connected. The electrical signal, being amplified twice, will be strong enough to turn on both the LED and the buzzer.

STEM Practice: Making a Humidity Sensor

Science	Know some basic electronic components;
Technology	Learn to assemble electronic components according to the circuit diagram;
Engineering	Be able to make a humidity sensor;
Mathematics	Know the sequence to assemble electronic components.

Objectives

1. To know what a transistor is.
2. To understand the function of the audion in a circuit.
3. To understand the working principles of a sensor circuit.
4. To know how the circuit can be used in other circuit engineering.

Materials

A base plate, screws, screw caps, wire connectors, a battery box (with batteries), barrier terminal block, a buzzer, an LED, transistor, resistor, wires, a plastic cup, metal sheets, plastic sheets, double-sided tapes.

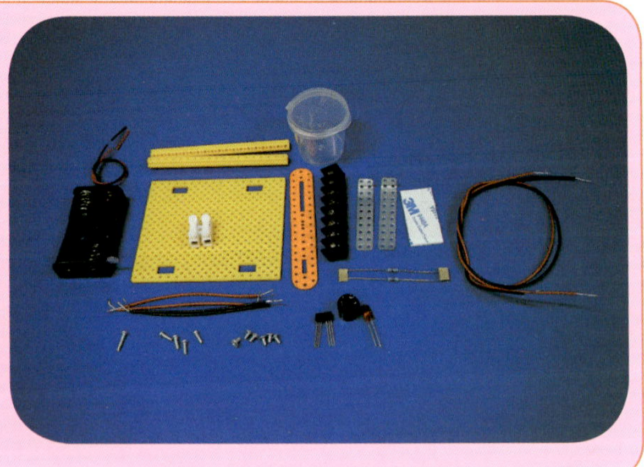

Process

1. According to Picture 1, install four 7 mm screws on the base plate.

2. According to Picture 2, fix the battery box on the base plate with 4 mm screws, and fix a white wire connector on the left side of base plate with 10 mm screws. Then place and fix the barrier terminal block on the upper part of the base plate with double–sided tapes.

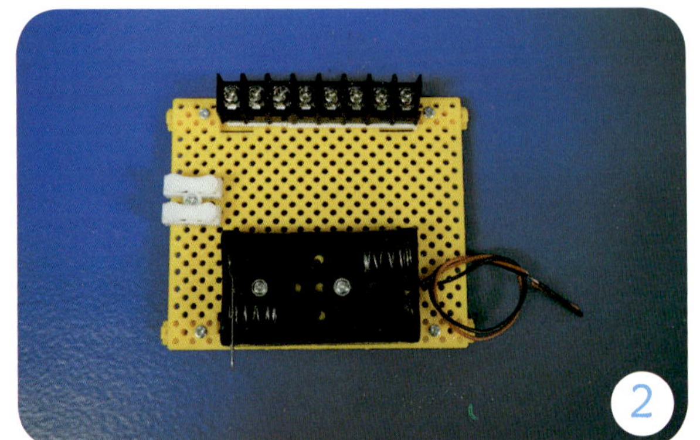

3. Observe the circuit diagram below. Remember to distinguish the positive from negative sides of the electronic components and learn how they are connected in the diagram.

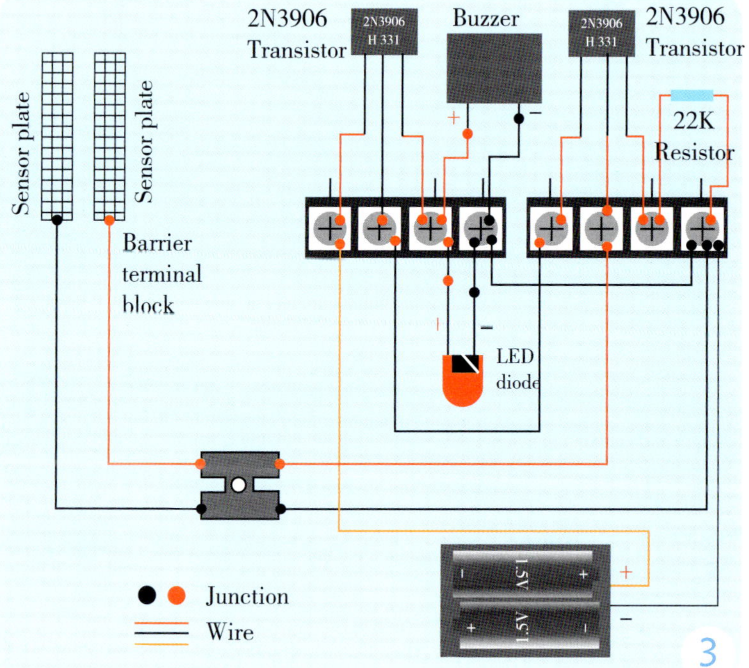

4. According to the circuit diagram, install the transistor on the barrier terminal block (with the letters facing up), then install the buzzer and LED on the barrier terminal block. Next, install the resistance and finish the circuit connection.

5. According to Picture 5, use 4 mm screws to install the metal sheets on the plastic sheet with the 40 cm red wire inserted under the screw.

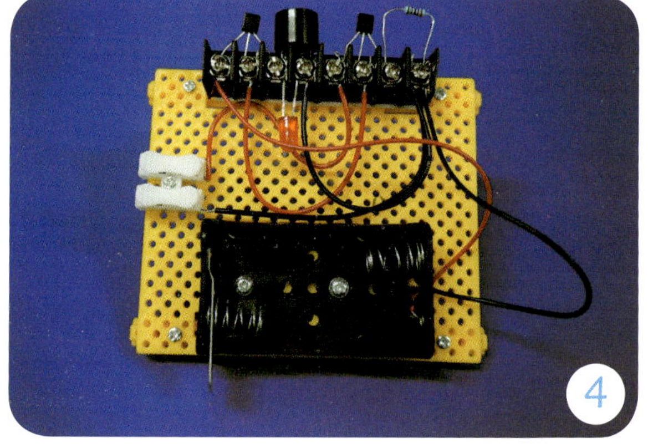

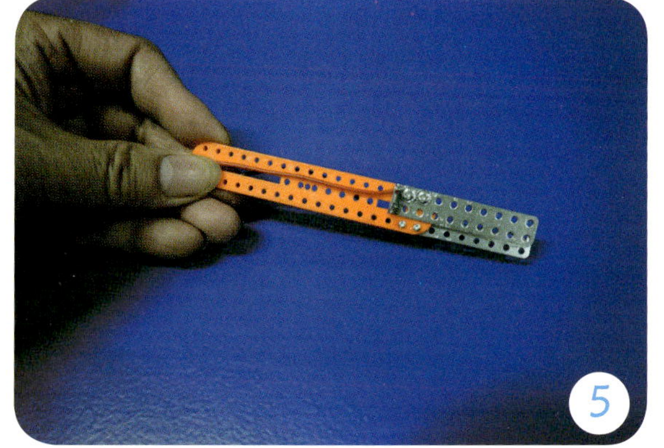

6. Do the same on the other side with the 40 cm black wire according to Picture 6.
7. Insert the red and black wires of the sensor into the white barrier terminal block and the humidity sensor is finished! Prepare a cup of water and put the sensor into the water. The LED turning on and the buzzer sounding signify the humidity sensor is under its regular working state.

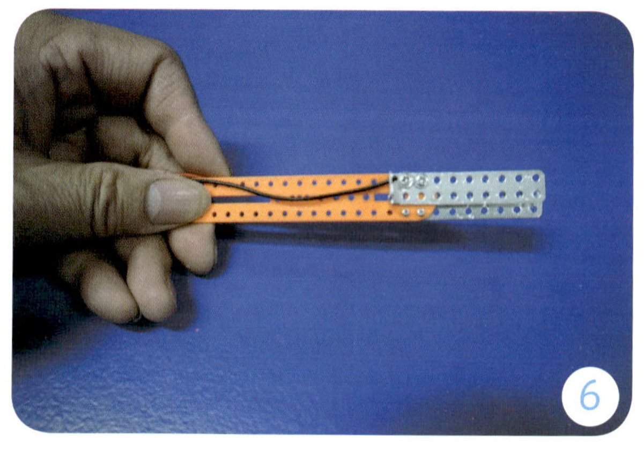
6

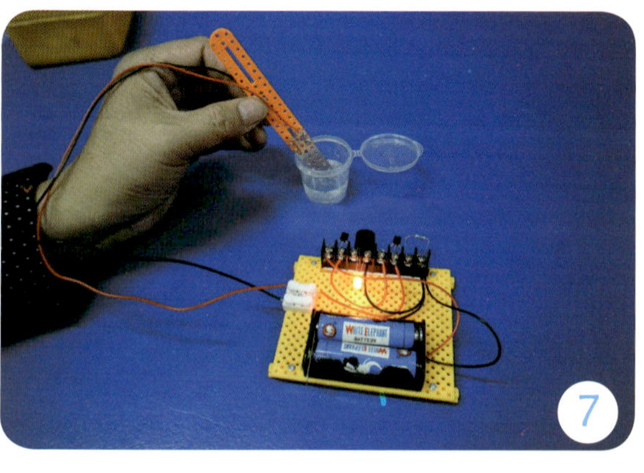
7

Extension

If you can add a different humidity-condition transducer, then you will be able to control when the LED will be on, and then, the humidity sensors will be even more useful.

Lesson 4 Acid-base Indicator

Solutions in daily life

We use many solutions in our daily life. Some of them are drinks, such as mineral water, soft drinks, fruit juice, and tea. Some are used for seasoning, like soy sauce and vinegar. Some are used for washing, like laundry detergent, hand sanitizer, mouthwash and other cleaning supplies. In addition, there are also some household medicine, such as iodine and eye drops.

Which of these daily solutions are acidic, which are basic alkaline, and which are neutral? How can we tell?

The acid-base indicator

There are three kinds of acid-base indicators: purple litmus test solution, colorless phenolphthalein test solution and pH test paper. All of them can help us to find out whether the solution is acidic, basic or neutral. The litmus test solution turns red combined with acid solution, blue with alkaline solution, and does not change color with neutral solution. This is a simple way to identify acid and alkaline solutions. The phenolphthalein test solution only turns red when reacting with an alkaline solution. So it can only identify alkaline solutions. The pH test paper is the most commonly used acid-base indicator, because it not only reveals the acidic, neutral or alkaline nature of the solution, but also shows the intensity of acidity and alkalinity.

So, how can we make our own acid-base indicator in daily life?

STEM Practice: Making an Acid–base Indicator

Science	Know how to use acid–base indicators to test the acidity or alkalinity of a solution;
Technology	Use common materials to make acid–base indicators and test the acidity or alkalinity of solutions with them;
Engineering	Make an acid–base indicator;
Mathematics	Understand concentration ratios and time control.

Objectives

1. To understand different types of acid-base indicator.
2. To know that the acid-base indicator participates in a chemical reaction with the solution; be able to tell the acidity or alkalinity of the solution (based on a change in color).
3. To make an acid-base indicator.
4. To use the self-made acid-base indicator to test unknown solutions.

Materials

Curry powder, alcohol, water, strips of white cloth, tweezers, plastic cups, sodium bicarbonate, a pipette, paper towels.

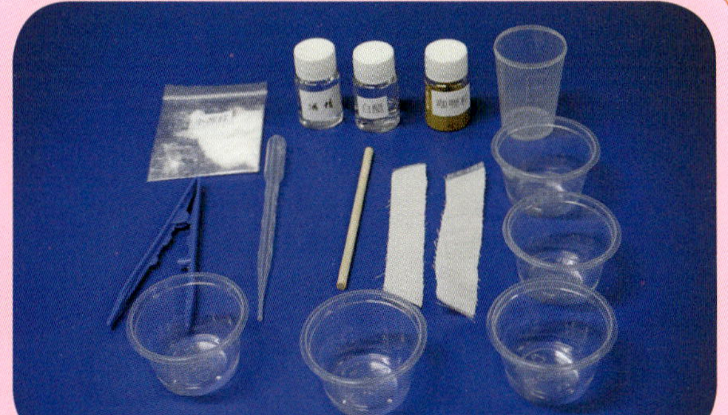

Process

1. Pour the curry powder into a plastic cup. Add some alcohol into the curry powder.
2. Mix the curry powder and alcohol to a paste.

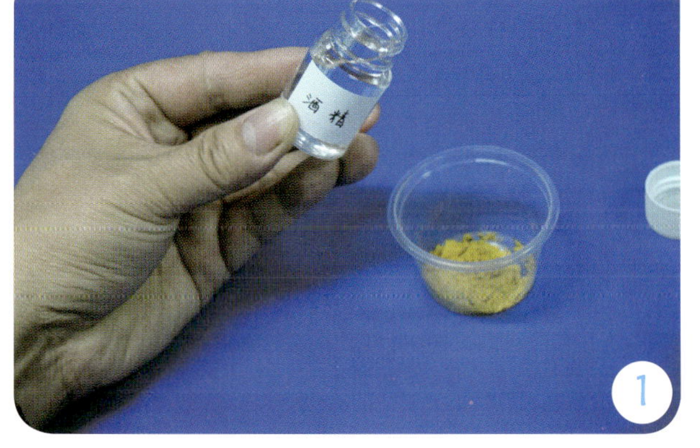

3. Immerse a strip of cloth in it, hold it still for a while, then take it out with tweezers. You will find that the color of the cloth has turned into yellow.
4. Take the cloth out and rinse the curry powder off its surface with water. Use paper towel to absorb water from the cloth. Let the cloth dry completely. A strip of yellow acid–base indicating cloth is done. Its color is yellow—the same as the pH test paper.

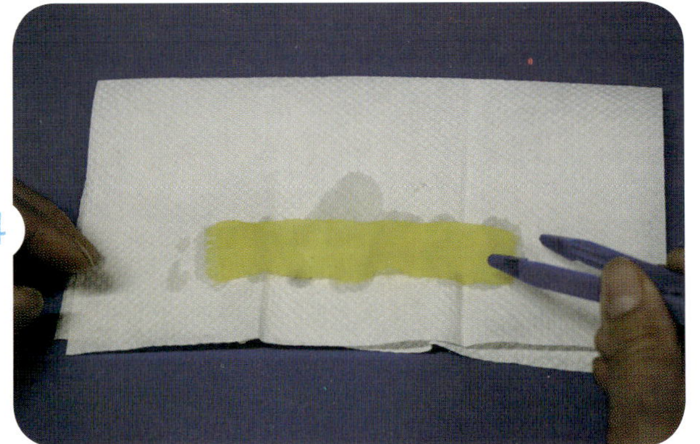

5. Pour some sodium bicarbonate and water into another plastic cup. Stir to make a sodium bicarbonate solution.

6. A drop of sodium bicarbonate solution will turn the color of the strip of cloth into light red, which indicates that the solution is alkaline. Such yellow strips can be used to check if the solution used at home is an alkaline solution.

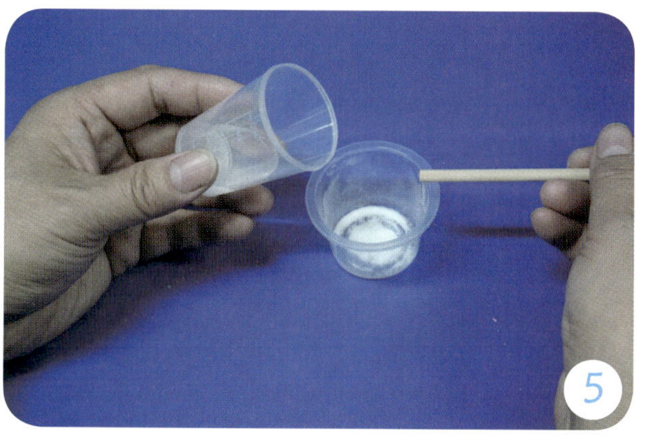

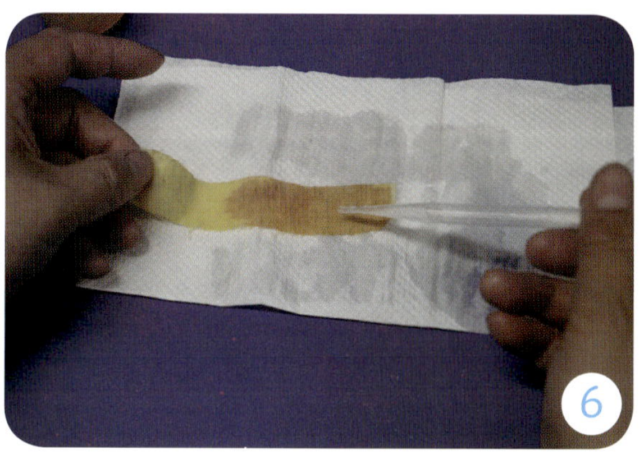

Extension

Use purple cabbage to make an acid–base indicator:

First, put diced cabbage in a container. Carefully add boiling water. Wait for 10 minutes until the water turns into purple. Remove the cabbage leaves, and put the water in a cup or a beaker.

Pour a moderate amount of water into two new cups or beakers. Pour some sodium bicarbonate (alkaline solution) into the first one and some white vinegar (acid solution) into the second one. When you add some of the purple cabbage water into each beaker, the color of the solutions will change. The first one (alkaline solution) will turn green while the second one (acid solution) red.

A solution of purple cabbage water works as an acid–base indicator as well.

Lesson 5 Windmill

History of wind energy

China is one of the earliest countries in the world to use wind energy. In ancient China, wind was used to set sail. The Chinese character "帆" (sail) can be found in the oracle bones, indicating that China has a long history of using wind energy. We use the wind to carry water, irrigate, grind rice and wheat and to sail. In Song Dynasty, vertical shaft windmills were widely used in China and are still in use today.

The use of wind in foreign countries is similar to that in China. It is worth noticing that the Dutch windmill is commonly used to draw water from lakes and low wetlands in the Rhine Delta, and it is also used for sawing wood and oil extraction. After steam engines invented, windmills gradually disappeared.

Wind turbines

We can see some really tall windmills, spreading over mountains, grasslands, sometimes even on the sea. They can be called turbine, or wind–driven generators. People use wind to rotate pinwheels as well as power generators.

Wind power stations should be built in places where wind is usually steady in all seasons, not too weak and not too strong (wind speed should be between 4 and 25 meters per second). It is worth noticing that, offshore wind power stations can be up to 7 times more efficient than the ones on land!

STEM Practice: Making a Pinwheel

Science	Uderstand the working principles of a rotating pinwheel;
Technology	Know the steps of making a pinwheel;
Engineering	Observe, make and test a pinwheel;
Mathematics	Find out the diagonal lines and center points on the paper.

Objectives

1. To find out how the rotating direction of the pinwheel is affected by the direction to which the blades are facing.
2. To find out how the angle of the blades affects the wind made by a electric pinwheel.
3. To find out how the number of blades affects the wind made by a electric pinwheel.

Materials

Paper, scissors, push pins, double-sided tapes, clips, straws, batteries, a battery box, a motor, plastic tires, a ruler.

Process

【 Activity 1 】Make a pinwheel

1. Fold the paper into a triangular shape and cut the extra part to form a square.

2. Fold the square along the two diagonals, then cut along the diagonals, but only halfway. Don't cut all the way through!

3. Pull four corners toward the center of the square one by one, in a counterclockwise order, and stick them with double-sided tapes.

4. Carefully poke a hole through the center of the pinwheel with the push pin.

5. Poke a hole on the straw.

6. Straighten a paper clip and use it to fix the pinwheel onto the straw by passing it through the two holes. Do not make the connection too tight. Make sure the pinwheel can rotate smoothly. Move the windmill back and forth to observe its rotation.

Tips

The principle behind rotation of the pinwheel:

The blades of the pinwheel are not in the same plane and can form slopes which will create a force of resistance when being blown by the wind. This will make the pinwheel rotate.

Activity 2: Investigate the relationship between the angles of the fan blades and the efficiency of the wind blown.

1. Draw two circles on cardboard and cut them out.
2. Draw two perpendicular lines that pass through the center of the circle with a ruler.

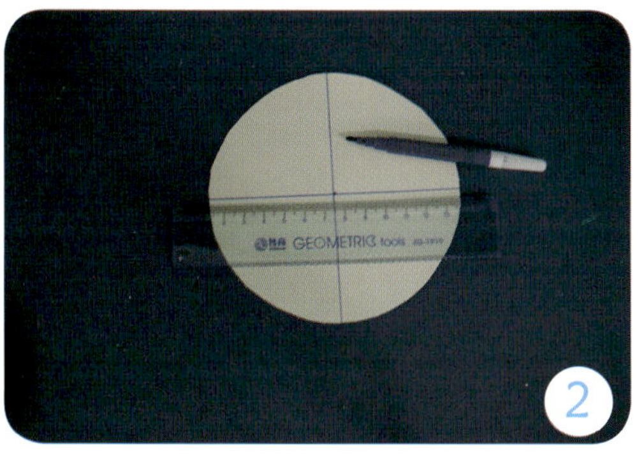

3. Cut the same length along each edge of the lines and fold the corners upwards with the same angle. Stick the side of the plastic tire onto the center of the circle using double-sided tapes.
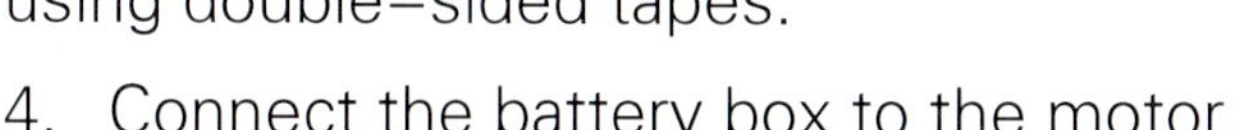
4. Connect the battery box to the motor.

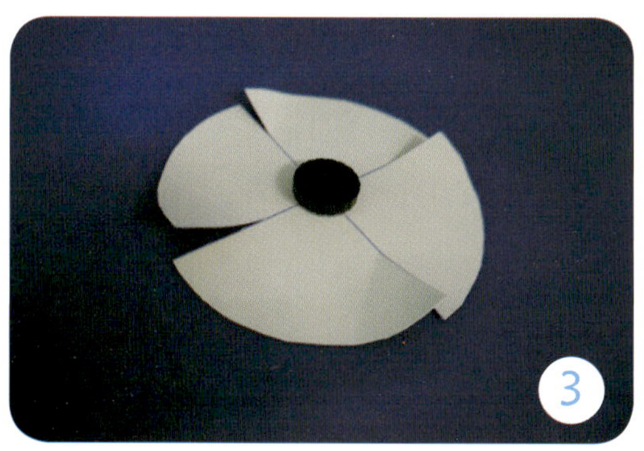

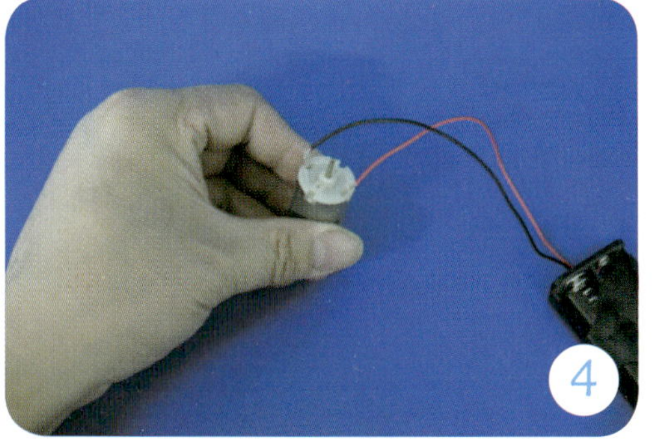

5. Insert the axle of the motor into the back of the tire and place the batteries into battery box. Test the speed and power of the wind created by the fan.

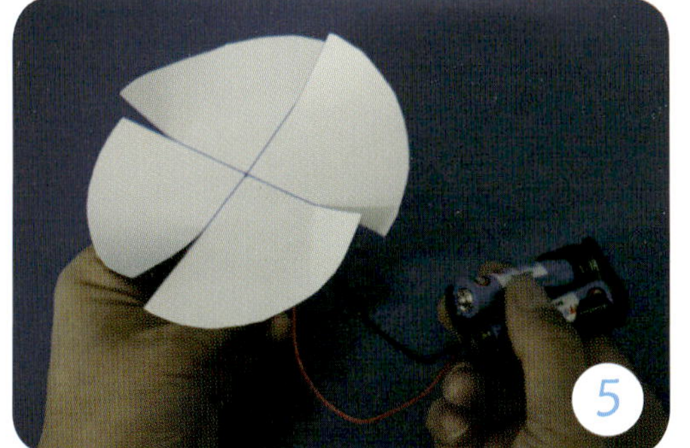

6. Adjust the angle of fan blades and explore the relationship between the angle of fan blades and the power of wind created by the fan.

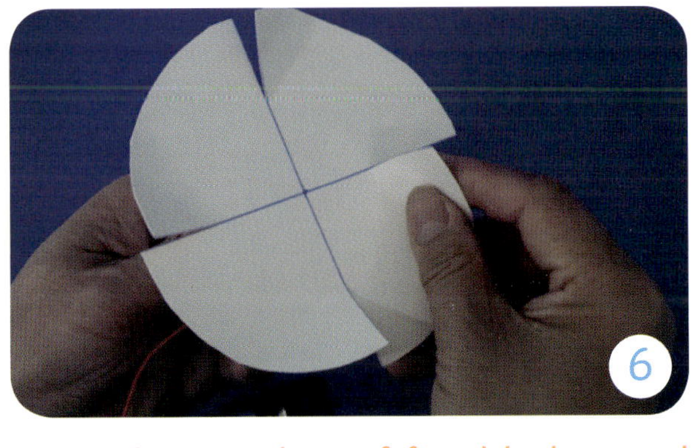

Activity 3: Figure out the relationship between the number of fan blades and the power of wind created.

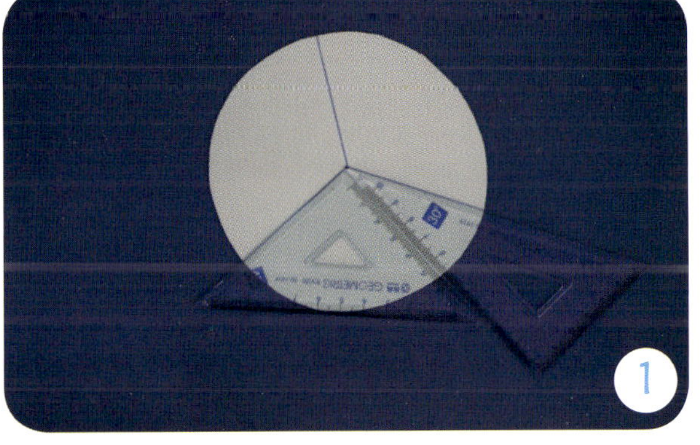

1. Use the triangle rulers to divide the circle into three equal parts.
2. Cut the circle into a three-bladed fan, according to the lines. Check the lines to make sure the cuts are symmetrical.
3. Connect the fan to the power source and figure out the relationship between the number of fan blades and the power of wind created by the fan.

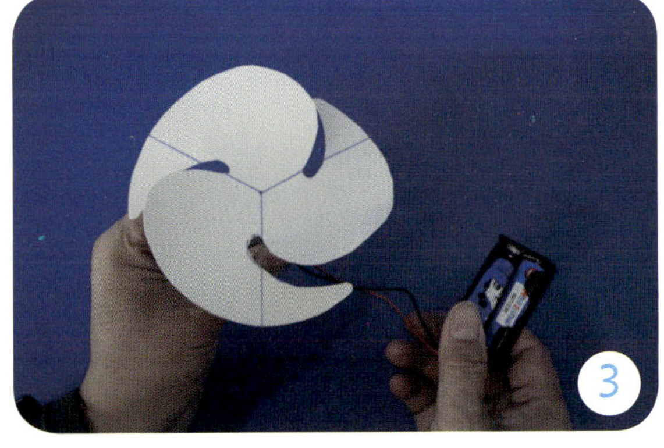

Extension

Wind energy is a clean energy source. Can you think of a way to convert wind energy into other forms of energy?

Lesson 6 Badminton

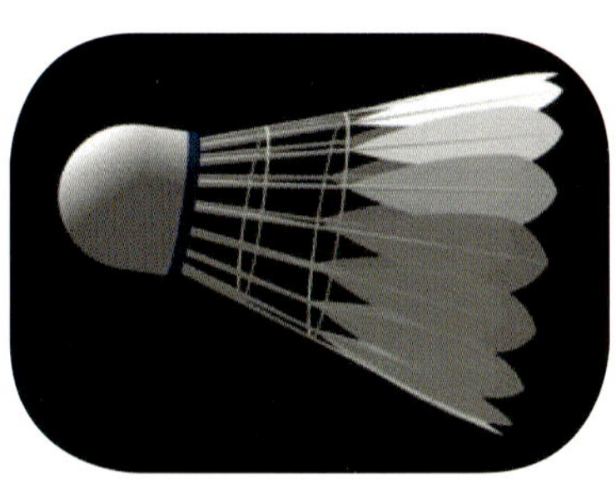

Badminton is a popular sport, enjoyed by many people all over the world. When the shuttlecock falls, does the cork base always hit the ground first? Let's uncover the working principles behind moving objects!

There may be several factors that affect how the shuttlecock flies and how it lands. We should consider things like the magnitude of the force (how strong is the strike, or the throw), the direction of the force (does the shuttlecock get hit diagonally or vertically), the material of the feather crown, and whether it is windy or not. You can work in three teams of four people, in which two would be responsible for playing badminton, while the other two would be observing and recording test results.

【Experiment】Make a shuttlecock and try to change two factors among the magnitude of the force, directions of the force, field size, weather and the material of the feather crown, each at a time during the play, to see how these changes will make a difference to the landing conditions of the shuttlecock.

【Pictures/Videos】Omitted

【Conclusion】According to the experiment, under the same conditions, no matter which factor get changed, the shuttlecock always touches the ground with its cork base first.

Why does the shuttlecock always touch the ground with its cork base first?

Observe the cork base and the feather crown, what are the differences between them? We can see they are made of different materials and have different shapes.

According to the kinematics, a falling object will spin and receive the resistance from the air at the same time. Because of the different materials and shapes, the air resistances force on the cork base and feather crown are also different. The air resistance forces on the feather crown is stronger than that on the cork base,

which make the cork base touch the ground first.

Are there other objects falling like shuttlecocks?

Many things in our life falling like the shuttlecock, such as cream cake, parachute and so on. Cream cake is made of cream and cake which have different materials and shapes. When a cream cake is falling, gravity center of the cream part is outside the whole cream cake, which will make it receive more resistance from the air. Thus, the cream part will touch the ground first. A Western proverb says, "The cream part always touches the ground first, when an entire cream cake is falling." What about the parachute? No doubt the person who wears the parachute can touch the ground before the parachute. Because the parachute receives more air resistance than a person, making itself falling slower than a person.

The less air resistance the objects receive, the faster they will touch the ground. If an object has two parts, the part that receives less air resistance will fall on the ground first.

Things like the cream cake will also change the way of falling on the ground. For example, if you throw a shuttlecock on the ground heavily, the feather part may touch the ground first; a stumbled moving object may change its moving trail or way of landing.

STEM Practice: Drawing and Making a Shuttlecock

Science	Know that during landing, the cork base will hit the ground first because it encounters smaller air resistance with a smaller contact surface;
Technology	Use materials such as plastic bottles, ping-pong balls and foam sheaths to make a shuttlecock;
Engineering	Make a shuttlecock;
Mathematics	Learn to draw the three-dimensional diagrams of a shuttlecock.

Objectives

1. To investigate the scientific principles behind the flying of the shuttlecock. To work on the exploring process consisting of asking questions, thinking, coming up with hypotheses and plans to test them.
2. To use both stick figure (which trains students'ability of describing things) and three-view drawing (which introduces the normative way of drawing) to illustrate the shape of a shuttlecock. To find their advantages and disadvantages.
3. To use multiple materials and methods (including cutting, filling, rotating, pricking) to make a shuttlecock. Test and see their overall performance.

Activity 1: Simple 2D drawing

【Drawing】Look at the pictures and learn to draw a badminton shuttlecock.

【Writing】Conclude the steps of drawing according to the pictures.

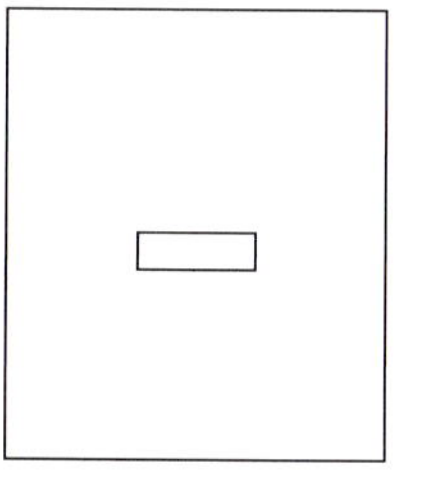
Draw a rectangle

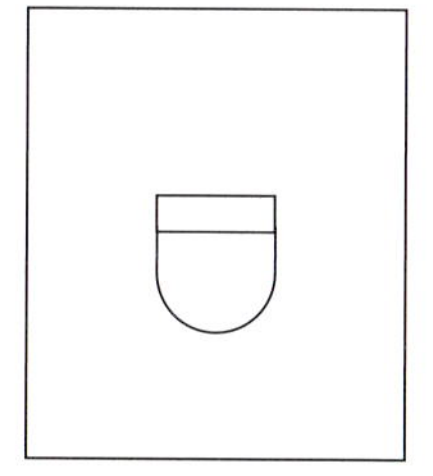
Draw a round bottom below the rectangle

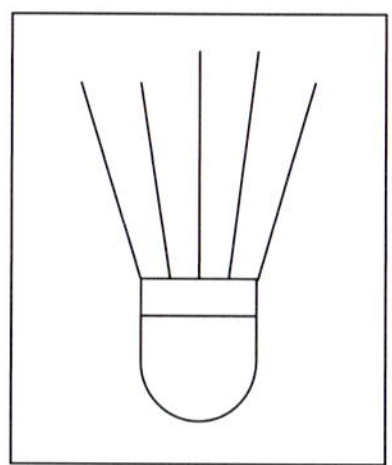
Draw five lines above the rectangle

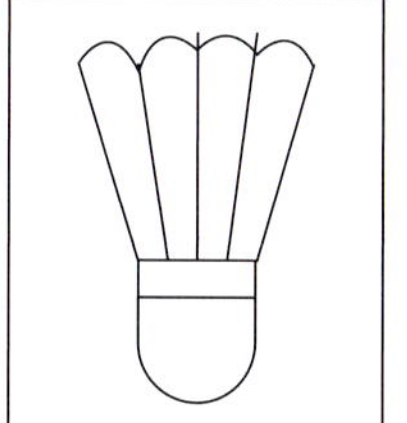
Draw four downward parentheses

Activity 2: Make a shuttlecock

Materials

Table tennis balls, push pin, scissors, a plastic bottle, foam mesh, hot glue, a candle, clay, double-sided tapes, etc.

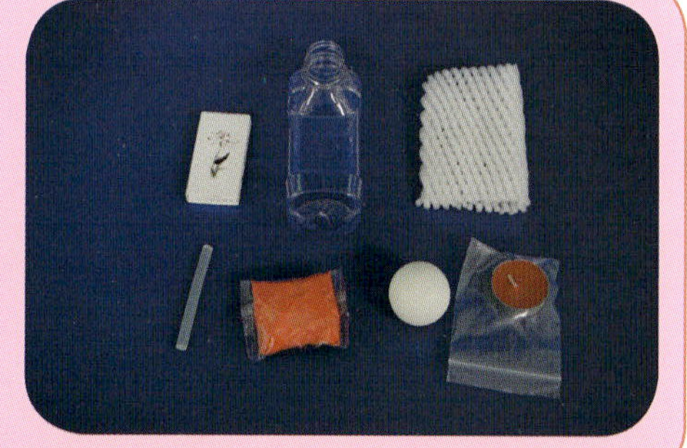

Process

1. Make a hole on a table tennis ball with a push pin.
2. As is shown in Picture 2, insert the scissors into the hole and cut apart the ball. Make the opening a little bigger than the mouth of the plastic bottle.

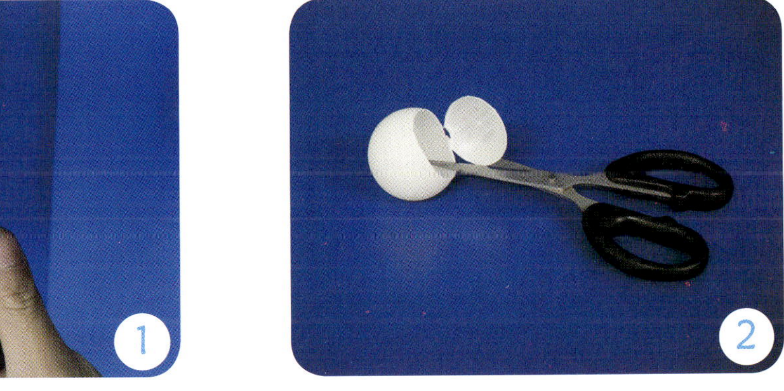

3. As is shown in Picture 3, cut the plastic bottle apart and take the front part.
4. Insert the mouth of the bottle into the prepared table tennis ball.

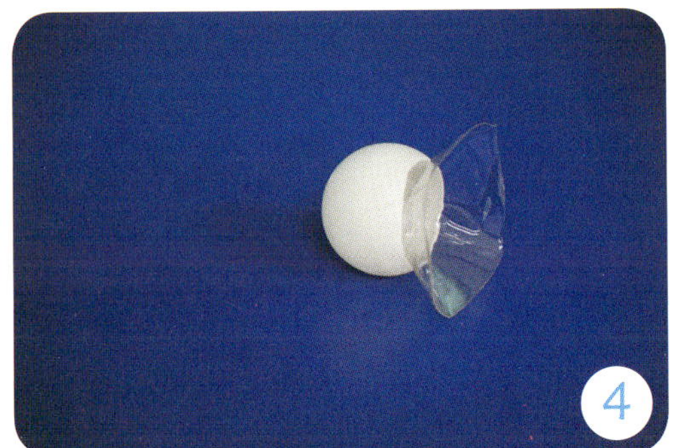

5. Melt the hot glue with the candle flame to connect the two pieces above.

6. Wrap the connecting area from outside using double-sided tapes.
7. Stick foamed plastic mesh around the outer side of the table tennis ball. Cut any redundant parts with scissors.

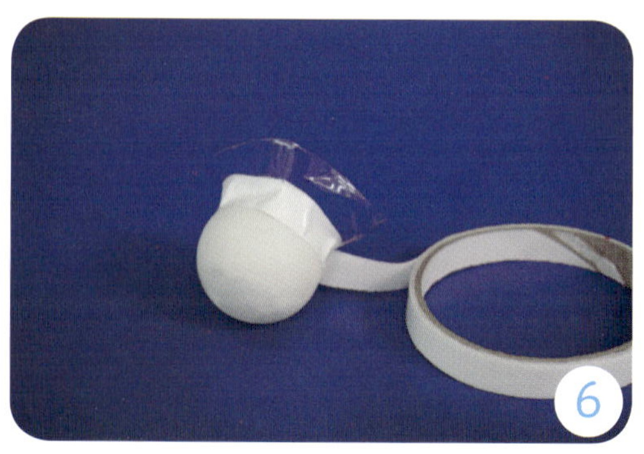

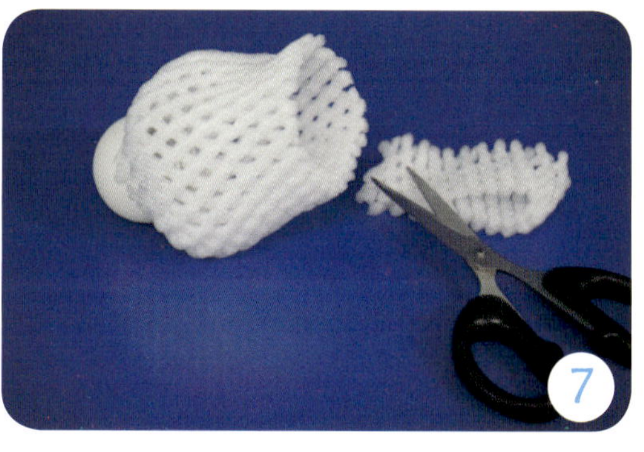

8. Cut the foam mesh into strips to simulate the feather crown of a shuttlecock.
9. Add clay inside the ball to finish the shuttlecock. You can change the amount of clay inside to test the movement of the shuttlecock.

Extension

Use your home-made shuttlecock to play a badminton match! Basic match rules (singles):

The player who first reaches 21 points wins a game. The first player to win 2 games (best of 3) would be the final winner of the competition. In each game, if there is a tie at 20 points, the winner must get an advantage of 2 points. If there is a tie at 29 points, the first one reaches 30 points wins the game.

Lesson 7 Wireless Remote Control Car

Based on Maxwell's electromagnetic theory, the radio communication technology was firstly used in navigation. People used Morse code to make sea–land communication.

Nowadays, remote control systems based on radio technolgy are widely used in military, domestic and medical areas, ranging from children's toys to warcrafts. The effective distance of these remote control systems can range from a few meters to tens of thousands of kilometers!

What is a radio remote control system?

Radio remote control systems consist of three main parts which are transmitters, receivers and actuators. Transmitters include circuits for coding (writing) and transmitting (sending) information. Receivers are made up of the receiving antenna, a receiving circuit and a demodulation circuit. Actuators include a decoding circuit and an executing circuit.

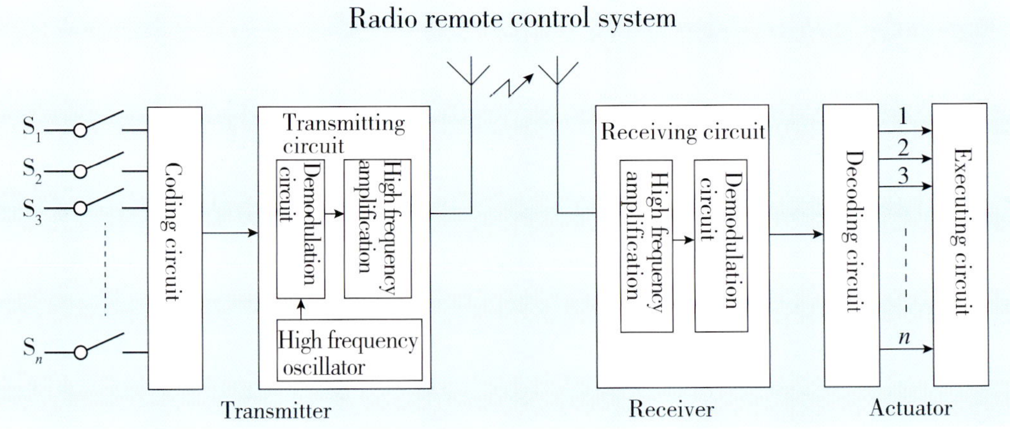

Receiving antenna turns the incoming radio wave into weak electrical signal.

After being selected and amplified by the receiving circuit, going through the process of demodulation, the instruction signal will be downloaded. The instruction signals are mixed together, so they need to be decoded (untangled) by a decoding circuit before being transmitted down to the executive circuit. Executing circuit will amplify the instruction signal, making the signal strong enough to operate the actuators. Thus, the object can be controlled.

As for actuators, they are devices that can respond to the instructions. They could be all sorts of devices: electromagnets that turned on, motors that rotating, valves that opened or closed, etc.

What is a coding circuit?

Coding happens in the transmitter, where the original signal will be processed under certain rules, in order to be more easily sent by radio waves. In other words, it is a process that changes one format of the message into another different one.

Frequency is often defined as the number of cycle in a second. For example, a signal of 1,000 Hz has 1,000 cycles in one second. Generally speaking, the signals from the coding circuit are relatively low in frequency, which makes it hard to be transferred directly to the target (the receiver). This means that these signals need to pass through a higher frequency carrier where they are modulated in order to be sent out successfully.

What is modulation?

Modulation means changing the information signal into a form which is more suitable for transmission. This can be done by changing the amplitude, phase, or frequency of the carrier signal. In general, it's better to change the information signals into a relatively higher frequency in accordance with the change of the carrier signal.

What is demodulation?

Demodulation is the opposite process of modulation. So it means that the

received signal will be transformed back into its original form, undoing the changes that were done to its frequency, amplitude or other properties.

What kind of wireless remote vehicle are we going to make?

The remote-controlled (RC) car we are going to make can move forward and backward. The maximum distance for control is about 4 to 5 meters. If there are two or more RC cars controlled by the same frequency of signal near each other, they will interfere with each other. The car may start spinning or moving unpredictably if it receives several signals with the same frequency.

STEM Practice: Making a Wireless Remote Control Car

Science	Learn about how radio waves work;
Technology	Learn about the process of assembling a remote control car;
Engineering	Assemble and test the wireless remote control car;
Mathematics	Measure the distance at which the car can be controlled.

Objectives

1. To assemble an RC car.
2. To control the RC car with a remote controller.
3. To understand the principles of remote control via radio signals.

Materials

A circuit board, a electric motor, eletric motor attaching clamp, a grid board, wheels, axle holder, antenna, axles, connectors, battery boxes, screws and so on.

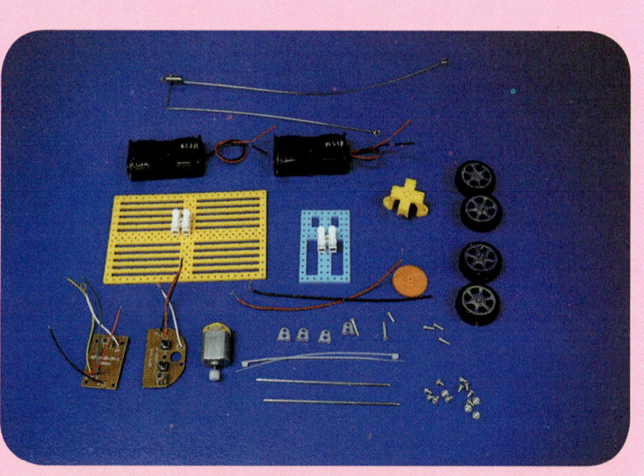

Process

1. Refer to Picture 1 and connect the green and yellow wires on the circuit board to the electric motor. Make sure there's no electrical power in your circuit yet.

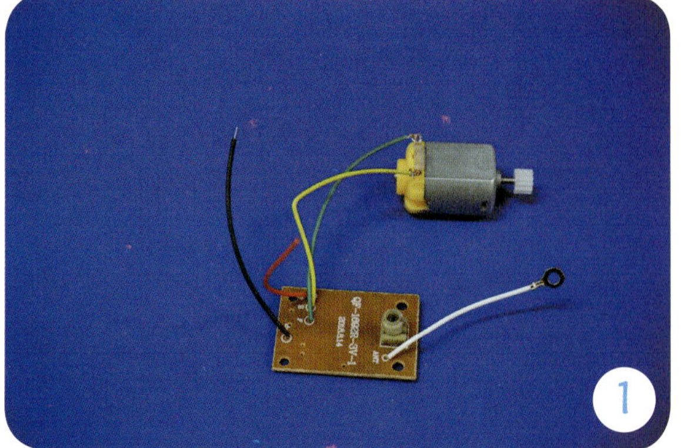

2. Look at Picture 2 and install four axle holders on the grid board with the 4 mm screws. Then install the wheels. The axles must go through the middle of the holes on the axle holders. Install the electric motor to the car frame with the attaching clamp and 7 mm screws.

3. Refer to picture 3 and fix the circuit board on the motor attaching clamp with 4 mm screws. Then insert the red and black wires of the circuit board into the connector. Fix the white connector on the car frame with a 12 mm screw. Connect the output wires of the battery box to connector respectively (red with red, black with black). Finally, fix the battery box on the vehicle frame with 4 mm screws.

4. Refer to Picture 4 and install the antenna with a 4 mm screw. The car is finished!

5. Refer to Picture 5 and install the remote control circuit board on the grid board with a 4 mm screw. Then install the antenna on the right side of grid board with a 4 mm screw. Next, install the connector on the left side of the grid board with a 12 mm screw. Finally, insert the red and black wires of the remote control circuit into the connector respectively.

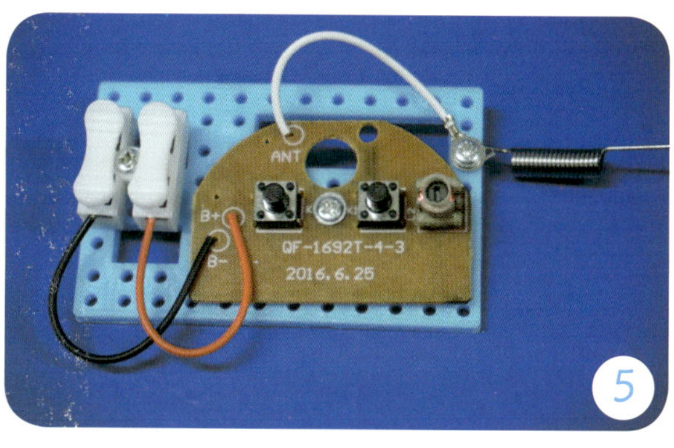

6. Refer to Picture 6 and install the battery box on the back of remote control circuit board with 4 mm screws and insert the output wires of the battery box into the white connector (red with red, black with black).

7. The whole system is completed. Install batteries and turn on the switch. Test your car, and see how well you can control it!

Extension

The wireless remote control car has been completed. You can then try using Bluetooth or APPs to control the car.

Lesson 8 Infrared Laser Alarm

A laser is the light emitted through a process of optical amplification based on the stimulated emission of electromagnetic radiation. The stimulated photon beam has the same optical properties and very high energy. With so much energy, lasers are also used for precise cutting, precise measurements, and for powerful lighting.

Einstein developed the theory of stimulated radiation in 1917. Ever after that, scientists had been working on it, until the discovery of laser, a breakthrough 43 years later. In 1964, Qian Xuesen, an well-known Chinese physicist, translated "laser" into "激光" formally.

Laser alarm is a typical application of laser. It is used as a passive reconnaissance equipment to detect enemy's laser weapons, laser guided weapons and laser radars. It usually consists of scanning antenna, laser detectors, amplifiers, microprocessors, instruction control units and alarm indicator.

How does an infrared laser alarm work?

This is a relatively simple device based on a combination of a pair of laser emitter and receiver. The infrared laser used in this device is linear and with no diffusion, which means it can be used to accurately hit a target. When the resistor is exposed to the laser, the resistance of it will become very small, resulting in a high conductivity in the circuit. In comparison, when the infrared laser is blocked, the resistance of the light-dependent resistor will increase rapidly, resulting in a very low conductivity in the circuit. Therefore, we can use those two different cricuit currents to control the transistor-based part of the circuit and the alarm.

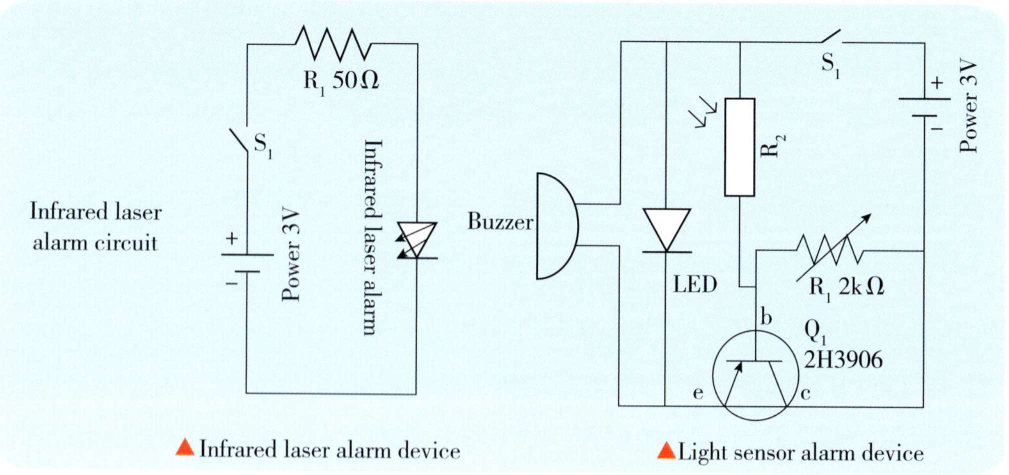

▲Infrared laser alarm device

▲Light sensor alarm device

How does our laser infrared alarm work?

In this model, we use the PNP triode to control the circuit. When the resistor is constantly exposed to the laser, the resistor will provide a positive current for b pole. At the same time, access between the e pole and c pole is cut off. Both the LED and the buzzer do not work. But when the laser is blocked, the resistance of light dependent resistor will increase, leading to a decrease of positive current, which eventually becomes smaller than the negative current. This turns on the access between the c pole and e pole, making the LED and buzzer start to work. The b pole is then acting as a switch, controlling the direction of the current.

How to protect the transistor from being damaged by excessive current?

To limit the current, we can add a resistor at the b pole. In the circuit, the positive pole is connected to the photoresistor, while the negative pole is connected to the adjustable resistor, both of which can reduce the current of b pole.

What kind of infrared laser alarm we are going to make?

In this model, we use PNP transistor to control the circuit. The photoresistor provides the transistor with a positive current when the laser beam lighting on it. The current from e pole to c pole is disconnected, LED and buzzer don't work.

When the laser beam is blocked, photoresistor's measurement will increase.

The negative current at the b pole is stronger than positive current, making e pole and c pole are connected, LED and buzzer start working. In this transistor circuit, b pole is a switch for controlling the directions of current.

How to use the laser alarm?

1. Single linear wiring

Let the infrared ray from the laser light directly on the photoresistor of the sensor alarm.

2. Multi–linear reflective wiring

Use small mirrors as reflection points to create zig–zagging paths for the infrared beam, before finally reaching the sensor. Through refraction, you may also create multiple infrared beams.

STEM Practice: Making an Infrared Laser Alarm

Science	Know about the working principles of an infrared laser alarm;
Technology	Learn to build an infrared laser alarm;
Engineering	Build an infrared laser alarm;
Mathematics	Learn to calculate the effective distance of the alarm.

Objectives

1. To install laser infrared alarm.
2. To understand the working principles of the infrared laser alarm.
3. To calculate and optimize the effective distance and placement of the infrared ray and alarm system.

Materials

Grid boards, L-shaped boards, poles, connectors, a buzzer, diodes, transistors, an adjustable resistor, a photoresistor, battery cases, battery, barrier terminal block, laser head, double-sided tape, metal screws (a screwdriver needed).

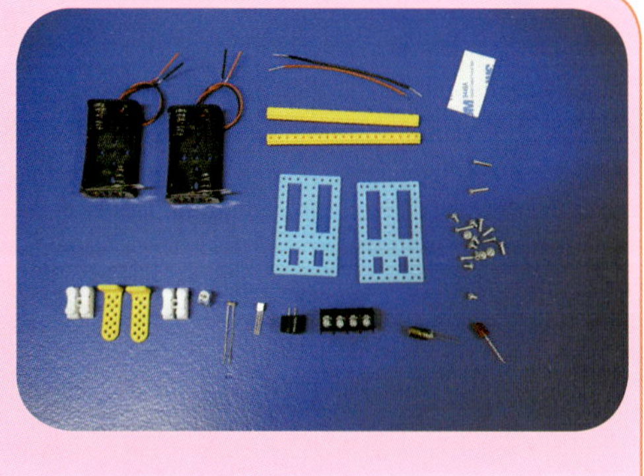

Process

1. Look at Picture 1 and install the L-shaped corners on the grid boards with 4 mm screws. Then install the short poles on the L-shaped corners with thick screws. Install the connectors on the top of the poles with 10 mm screws. Do not fix the screws too tight, and leave some room for further adjustment.

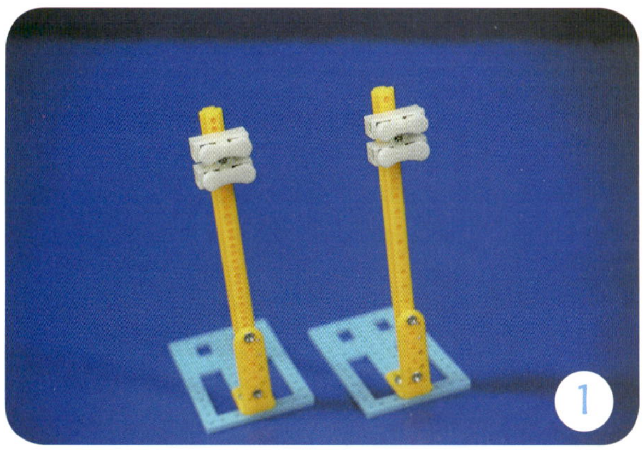

2. Read the circuit diagram. Be aware of the placement of the adjustable resistor and find out all its three pins. The proper method of using this adjustable resistor is to connect either pin 1 & 2 or 2 & 3 into the circuit, otherwise it won't work.

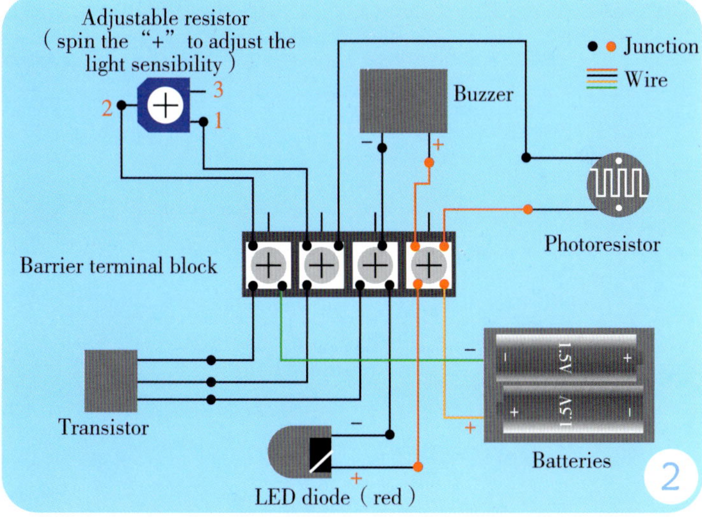

3. Refer to Picture 3 and the circuit diagram to correctly install the wires and components. The letter side of transistor must be facing up, and only connect two pins among three pins of the adjustable resistor, The buzzer and LED both have negative and positive pins that need to be distinguished. Connect their long pins to the positive pole, and their short pins to the negative pole. The buzzer's sticker must be removed after installation.

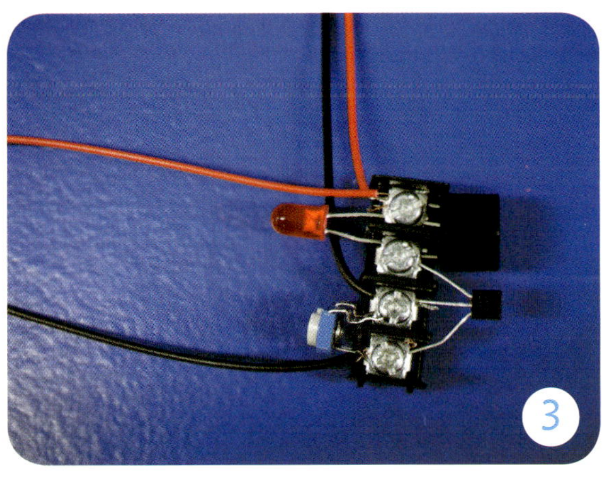

4. Refer to Picture 4, install the battery box onto the grid board with 4 mm screws. Then paste a small piece of double-sided tape on the pole to fix the small circuit board. Paste the connectors onto the pole with double-sided tapes. Then insert the red and black wires into the connector respectively.

5. Refer to Picture 5 and connect the photoresistor with the connector. Place the resistor parallel to the pole. The alarm section is now finished!

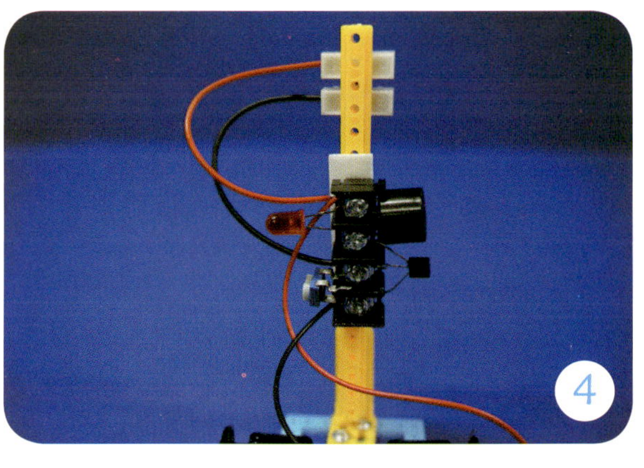

6. Install the battery case on the grid board with 4 mm screws, and then insert the output wires of the battery case into the connector.

7. Insert the laser head into the connector with the long pin connecting to the red wire and the short pin connecting to the black wire. The infrared beam section is now finished.

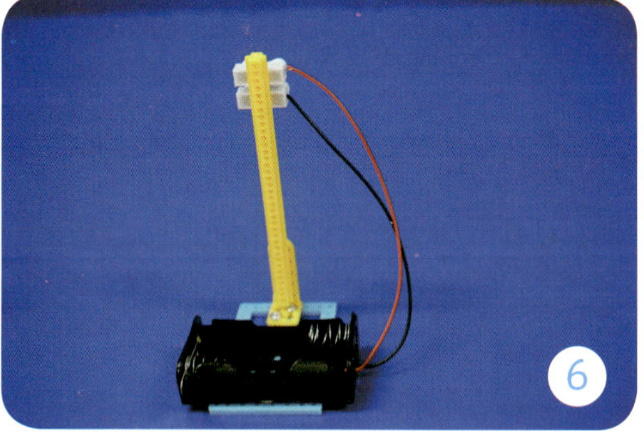

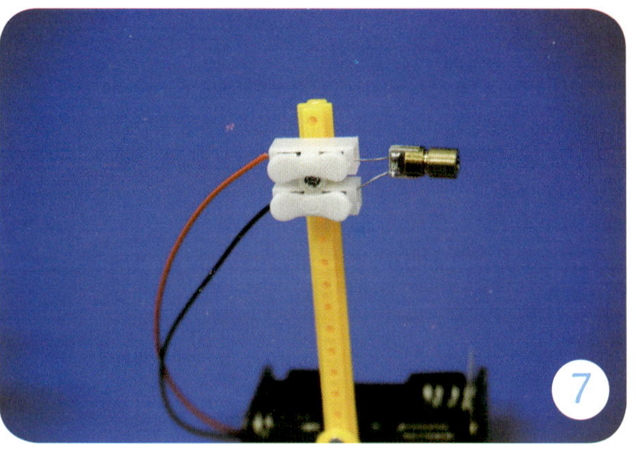

8. Install batteries for both sections, and close the circuits by turning down the switch in the battery cases. Adjust the position of the beam section to make sure the infrared laser is able to light directly onto the resistor. Notice that, after switching on the power, both the LED and the buzzer will immediately turn on, and will shut off only when laser is hitting the sensor. Calibrate the position of the laser and the resistor to stop the buzzing and set the system up for regular working conditions. If the buzzer doesn't stop buzzing, use a screwdriver to adjust the adjustable resistor. If the buzzer and LED can not be turnd on at all, check if all components are correctly installed.

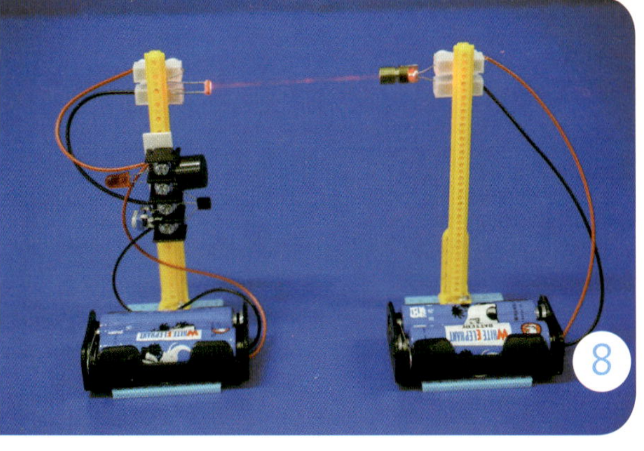

Extension

Can you try and see if the laser alarm has a distance limit?